A Lean Six Sigma Recipe: Improving a Process in a matter of months

Antonella Zompa

Published and printed by KDP in the United States of America

Credit for editing this book to Thomas M. Abbott, EdD.
Credit for cover design to Kate Lee.
Credit for reviewing this book Rebecca Bompiedi.

Portions of information contained in this publication/book are printed with permission of Minitab, LLC. All such material remains the exclusive property and copyright of Minitab, LLC. All rights reserved.

Disclaimer: The author makes no representations or warranties with respect to the accuracy or completeness of the contents of this work and specifically disclaim all warranties, including without limitation warranties of fitness for a particular purpose. No warranty may be created or extended by sales or promotional materials. The advice and strategies contained herein may not be suitable for every situation. It is sold with the understanding that neither the author nor the publisher is engaged in rendering legal, accounting, or other professional services. If legal advice or other expert assistance is required, the services of competent professional person should be sought. Further, readers should be aware that internet websites listed in this work may have changed or disappeared between when this work was written and when it is read.

Trademarks: All trademarks are the property of their respective owners. The trademarks that are used are without any consent, and the publication of the trademark is without permission or backing by the trademark owner. All trademarks and brands within this book are for clarifying purposes only and are owned by the owners themselves, not affiliated with this document.
Six Sigma is a federally registered trademark of Motorola, Inc.

ISBN 978-1-7347123-0-8 paperback

www.azconsulting-sp.com

Table of Contents

Foreword

I decided to write down the recipe that I have successfully used countless times during my career. I believe that there is always a solution to a problem and that continuous improvement embraces change to its core. This recipe has been proven effective for myself, my past employees, clients, and my current students.

This book follows a sequential logic, utilizing the DMAIC (Define-Measure-Analyze-Improve-Control) framework and tying one method to the next to actually improving a process using the Lean Six Sigma (LSS) philosophy. LSS is a hybrid formed from Lean (looking at Waste in your process) and Six Sigma (looking at variation in your process). Keep in mind there are many books on Lean Six Sigma. What makes this book different is that it takes only certain methods & tools from the LSS collection and puts them in a certain order to apply on an existing process at your workplace in order to enhance its efficiency. Therefore, do not think of this book as a laundry list of Lean Six Sigma's methods & tools. You can easily go find this information in a bookstore, library or on the internet at any given point.

For this book to work for you, follow the project selection criteria set out in the beginning of this book. Once you have your process selected, use this book as your guide walking you through step-by-step until you reach your future improved state. Consider this book more of a manual, where you are following a specific formula to improve your existing process. The aspiration of this book is to use it as a manual to complete your first process improvement, then rely on it as a reference whenever you embark on future improvement projects at work.

DEFINE PHASE

You may have good intentions of wanting to improve your entire workplace but remember that you need to walk before you can run.

If you were planning to climb Everest, your first step may be to put together an exercise plan to get your endurance up. But more importantly, you should go see your doctor for a complete physical to make sure you actually can climb the mountain!

In this phase, you are going to right size and scope out your project.

Chapter 1: Introduction to Lean Six Sigma

Let us begin this book by going through the history of Lean and Six Sigma. As many of you are aware, the two disciplines started as standalone philosophies.

In the 1800's, Carl Frederick Gauss introduced the normal curve metric famously known to us as the "bell curve". This was the start of statistical analysis and can be linked to the inception of six sigma. During the same time period, there were problems in batching creating inventories at all stations along with possible rework and scrap at assembly level which yielded high costs internally and delays to the customer. In 1913, Henry Ford created the "Flow Production", moving his factory equipment in a consecutive sequence that started from raw materials to the finished automobile. In fact, he only had one-part number. This can be considered the beginning of Lean even though it was not called that at the time. Unfortunately, the customers started wanting variety and Ford's flow production lacked the ability for customize the automobiles.

So, in the 1920's, other automotive companies came into existence creating competition to Ford's model, claiming to supply many models with various options. While Ford had only one-part number for his entire assembly of an automobile, the competition created new part numbers for each piece due to customization. This caused longer lead times for customers along with increase cost for factory machinery, which was required. Thus, the MRP or Material Requirements' Planning was born.

Then in the 1930's, Toyota engineers looked at innovating to keep with customer products' desires and continuous flow, introducing self-monitoring machines checking for quality. They called it Total Production System (TPS) where everything they do starts and ends with the customer. Based on the customer's needs, the goal is to create a continuous flow, eliminating any waste that impedes the flow to get the final product to the customer. Moreover, this is why Toyota is famous for creating the "Lean" philosophy.

On the Six Sigma end, Walter Shewhart depicted how three sigma deviation from the mean required a process correction also known as "Statistical Process Control" creating Control charting and adding to the bell curve idea.

Now what is interesting is that Walter Shewhart also dabbled in some concepts within the Lean philosophy. He created the "Shewhart cycle" in the 1950's, which is known today as PDCA (plan-do-check-act). During the same time frame, Juran and Deming were introducing the human aspect being important in the overall quality and contributed to the TQM (Total Quality Management) as well as Statistical Process Control approaches. They have been given credit for turning around the Japanese automobile industry prior to Lean. As time went by, in the early 1980's, Motorola engineers saw that measuring defect in the thousands of opportunities was not enough granularity and so introduced DPMO (defects per million opportunities). They created the new standard with a methodology and trademarked the words "Six Sigma".

In 1986, John Krafcik, while working on a MIT research project as part of the International Motor Vehicle Program, needed a name to call the Toyota's TPS phenomenon. The TPS philosophy was then changed to Lean and today many people know this methodology as Lean. And this is how the TPS acronym became the term Lean.

In 1990, a book called "The Machine That Changed the World" was written describing the Toyota way being more than just a methodology or a set of tools. It's about empowering individuals, continuously finding ways to improve daily and as a consequence, improving the company. Later in 1996, the authors came out with the best seller book "Lean Thinking."

In 1995, Jack Welch launched an initiative by focusing on the customer, enabling e-business, and thus adopting the statistical approach for GE (General Electric). They trademarked it as 6δ ™ methodology. He recruited Motorola's Mikel J. Harry, who is considered one of the fathers of Six Sigma to train the first class of Master Black Belts in GE.

In the early 2000's, companies went with either Lean or Six Sigma philosophies, depending mostly on leadership's decision-making. Slowly though both philosophies were seen as game changers within their own right. Six Sigma focuses on statistical variation and how to remove it from the process ensuring no defects while Lean focuses on removing waste and creating a continuous flow process. As these companies embraced both philosophies, Lean Six Sigma was introduced as the better of two worlds.

Thus, Lean Six Sigma is considered a hybrid, choosing from both Lean and Six Sigma toolkits in order to resolve the problem and satisfy the customer. Though there is no unique creator of Lean Six Sigma, we can consider Walter Shewhart as the grandfather since he created tools for both Lean and Six Sigma methodologies during his career.
As mentioned earlier, the two philosophies differ where Lean is about removing waste and improving efficiency while Six Sigma looks at reducing variation with a statistical-driven approach.

Yet they both also have similarities. For instance, both philosophies:

- believe that it's all about the customer.
- were initiated within the manufacturing sectors and later brought in for office and service improvements.
- are considered quality based and look at continuous improvement.

As you can see from the triangle, people come first; followed by the process and tools they use to accomplish their tasks. Lean Six Sigma is not about downsizing, eliminating jobs or removing fewer effective people. It is about empowering people with the necessary processes and tools, so they are skilled to do the job effectively.

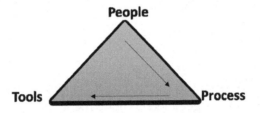

This is also not a top-down or bottom-up approach; it is both. In order to be successful in an organisation, there needs to be organic growth with a DNA mindset within all employees. Basically, it's a cultural change. Tools and methods alone will not turn an organization into Lean Six Sigma (LSS) mindset. It's all about working smarter, not harder! We are going to end this chapter by highlighting each of the philosophy's strengths.

1.1 SIX SIGMA

In Six Sigma, some key concepts are:

- Enables world-class quality and continuous improvement achieving customer satisfaction.
- Looks into reducing the variation of the process using data and establishes new standard of excellence at only 3.4 DPMO.

The statistical software used in this book will be Minitab®. Instead of manually calculating the statistical reports that address variation, Minitab® will do the calculating for you and you will be required simply to interpret your results. Refer to the Minitab® Step-by-Step Guide which complements this book and is found in Appendix A.

The methods and tools may differ depending on whether you want to improve a process or redesign one altogether. Improving goes through the DMAIC framework where:

Define – what is/are the customer need(s) of the existing process?
Measure – what is/are the defect(s) and what is its frequency of occurrence?
Analyze – when, where and why the defect(s) occur?
Improve – how can we fix the process and reduce/eliminate the defect(s)?
Control – how do we maintain the process with the fix(es)?

NOTE: If fixing a process really means you want to redesign the process from scratch or you need to establish a new process because it is lacking, the DMAIC framework will not work as well as the DFSS (Design for Six Sigma) methodology. In this methodology, there are various frameworks developed by companies internally to satisfy their needs. We are not touching DFSS in this book. This book will focus on improving an existing process at your workplace using this DMAIC framework.

1.2 LEAN

While utilizing the framework from the Six Sigma philosophy, we are going to be incorporating Lean principles to target and eliminate the waste in the process as well. You are going to be looking at the types of waste, the "5S plus Safety" (found in Chapter 28) concept of organizing from chaos, going to "Gemba" (found in Chapter 17) to understand exactly what is occurring in your process, mapping out your results as a "Value Stream Map or VSM" (found in Chapter 19) and looking at the value-add versus non-value added tasks within the process. If this sounds all alien to you, do not worry, it will become clearer as we progress in our journey of fixing your process.

Once you understand the problem and have analyzed its root causes, then you can effectively use Shewhart's cycle or PDCA (Plan-Do-Check-Act) framework to put in place a better future state process.

Think of Lean as being a structured approach to shift your way of thinking in continuous improvement. In fact, while Six Sigma will deal mostly with mathematics to show defects, Lean will deal with paradigm shift in your thinking when looking at a process. A great article published by Harvard Business, "Learning to Lead at Toyota" writes about how a high-level position starting at Toyota to get acclimated to the Lean DNA. This article highlights how each employee entering Toyota, regardless of their level of seniority, need to go through the basics in Lean to understand the company's DNA.

Keep in mind, both philosophies require a mindset where the company adopts them as part of their make-up or DNA. You can start the paradigm shift by showing them how you learned and put in practice this hybrid philosophy in your workplace.

Chapter 2: Project Selection

When selecting the right project, you need to be aware of the type of problem you are trying to resolve. If the problem has possible answers or you can easily get the answers by asking the right people, then consider it a quick hit resolution. If you think of a tree analogy, its fruit on the ground you just need to pick. The next level, or low hanging fruit can be when your issue requires you to get people in a room to brainstorm ideas to change for the better, consider it as conducting a kaizen; or if your issue is, chaos and you need to organize your space using the 5S plus Safety method. Once again, you can just do it!

Now if you have a problem on an existing process, product or service, you need to fix it or improve it, and neither quick hits nor the low hanging fruit methods will work, then you will go through a DMAIC project. In some cases, you may have the solutions, but you need to test them out, you may skip DMAIC, conduct a continuous improvement method called Kaizen (found in Chapter 29 to remove Waste, and test it using the PDCA method (found in Chapter 26). But if you are lacking the solutions or unsure, want to look into the variation of your process and require to root-cause, then this is when you decide to use DMAIC framework.

Remember that when you are selecting a project, it needs to follow the SMART acronym! Let us go through each of the letters to breakdown your problem and ensure if can be a project you can use DMAIC framework for.

"S" stands for Specific: You begin by being specific about the project and answering the What? Why? Who? When? Where? Which? Also, when you are answering the questions, do not only think about your needs but also the customer's. In LSS, the philosophy is working on things that impact the customer. Thus, it always starts and ends with the customer.

"M" stands for Measurable: Identify the defect or defects of your problem and quantify them. Six Sigma using statistical analysis, so data on your existing process is going to be required.

"A" stands for Attainable: For attainable, answer the questions: Is your project able to attain the required expertise and resources it requires? Do you respond to your customers' requirements? Make sure everything and everyone is in your reach.

"R" stands for Realistic: Make sure your project is manageable by asking yourself: Is it realistic for you to tackle the scope you have specified balancing your life and daily work routines?

"T" stands for Timely: You want to make sure you can complete the project within the time allotted. In this book, we will follow a recipe that if completed weekly, you can improve your process within three months.

2.1 Know your Customer

So, who is the customer? Many people think it's the external end customer, the one who buys your finished goods. But when we look at LSS projects, our customers can also be internal. Basically, the customer is who is voicing their concerns on an existing process and want it to improve. Thus, for a DMAIC project, the customer:

- Has given feedback on a problem, issue or improvement needed which relates to your job
- The process exists in-house and you are allowed to improve it
- You will be able to get your project team the required resources to help you improve the process

The customers are the recipients of your process' output. Some examples of what internal and external customers look like are:

Internal Customers:
- Departmental
- Manager
- Sponsor
- Factory floor
- Office

External Customers:
- End user
- Supplier
- Consumer
- Contractor
- Partnership

Once you identified who your customer is, you are going to collect their needs, wishes and desires. We are going to call the feedback you collect: VoC or Voice of the Customer. Here are some examples of VoC:

- you attended a meeting and heard that your department's process is slow for the hundredth time.
- you receive complaints by email or phone calls.
- your department's dashboard or scorecards is showing RED because it's not meeting its target.
- you see all the money spent on scrap & rework costs or non-compliances
- you spent your days figuring out who can help you solve a customer issue

Think of your VoC as the main reason why you are embarking in a DMAIC project. At the end of the day, you will need it to make management understands the importance of having you spend time with a team correcting the problem. Therefore, customer feedback is something you can measure at the beginning of the project and then at the end of the project to see if your improvements have satisfied your customer. In LSS, we look at what is important to the Customer and call it their CTQ (Critical to Quality). So, take the time to collect the VoC from your customer, probing on what is critical for them. You can use some of the following methods to collect your VoC:

- Benchmarking
- Business Dashboard or Scorecard
- Complaints
- Discussion
- Focus Groups
- Interviewing
- Surveying

So let us recap, you have a problem you believe is important to you, your team and to the customer. You have collected the VoC to make your case. You now understand exactly what the customer deems important to them to get resolved. You are now ready to go through the project selection criteria. If at this point you are still wondering what type of project can go through a DMAIC framework in LSS, here are some examples that can jog your memory:

- Improve order entry cycle time
- Decrease the rework of a component
- Achieve customer responsiveness within 24 hrs.
- Improve accounts receivable
- Decrease scrap in the packaging department
- Reduce shipment damages
- Decrease site inventory
- Reducing project margin erosion

- On-time delivery on site
- Reducing cost of non-quality
- Reducing engineering submittals cycle time
- Improve cycle time for PODs (proof of delivery documents)

Do not limit yourself to these examples, there can be more than one out there specific to your company that can satisfy the selection criteria and use the DMAIC framework. Reach out to your manager and/or local quality person. In some cases, you may already have a Quality Office which includes Blackbelt (BB) and Master Black Belt (MBB) employees that can help you in problem identification.

2.2 Selecting the right Project

Here is the checklist you must use when selecting a process to improve. Remember you are still in the preliminary phase so once you scope it out you may find it's too big of a scope and only take a portion of the problem for your project. The key is to answer "YES" to all the questions below. This will give you a higher probability of selecting the right project for the DMAIC framework.

- Does the process exist?
- Is the process part of your job or something with which you are intimately familiar?
- Does the problem or one of the problems stem from the Customer(s)?
- Does your intended project hold a known problem(s)?
- Is this problem contained within one group or department you are part of?
- Does this problem have unknown causes where solution(s) cannot be pre-determined?
- Do you want to keep and improve this particular practice?
- There is no IT involvement for developing software?
- It is easy to gather data and information?
- Are you able to collect data for analysis of problem?
- Do you know the root cause to the problem?
- Do you have target benefit(s) for this project?

Chapter 3: Voice of the Customer (VoC)

We briefly touched this topic in our last chapter. In this chapter, we are going to go a little more in depth. Remember, in LSS it starts and ends with the customer. Therefore, the customer should be your main trigger for improving a process.

Who is my Customer? The person(s) who are the recipient of your product or service. Thus, if you are part of a process that is building a product, your customer may be the one paying your company for the work performed. In this example, you are going to have an external customer, which can be a consumer, supplier, end user or contractor. But if you are working on the product which then goes to another station / department, then your customer is going to end up being internal (i.e. the next station/department). Now if you are in operations putting together reports, your customer may end up being your manager or sponsor. They may want you to improve on the reports, for example making them more legible, easier to follow or visual. Regardless in this case your customer is internal.

It is important in LSS to identify your customer as you are identifying the process and problem you want to resolve. To give more power to your problem statement, you collect the VoC from your customer. This VoC is translated into your project's requirements or Customer-to-Quality, known as CTQs which are the attributes of what is critical to quality for the customer. The goal is to bring value to the customer, build key relationships, and possibly grow the business and identifying new opportunities. Fixing something that the customer believes is broken is a great way of gaining the loyalty of your customer.

So, if we recap, the three steps are:

1. Who is my Customer? Note: The person(s) who are the recipient of your product or service
2. Collect VoC data to better understand the impact
3. Translate the VoC to critical to quality (CTQ) attributes

Now there are several methods of collecting the VoC from your customers. You can be proactive or reactive.

Proactive methods mean you are taking the initiative to collect VoC:

- interviewing (call them up or meet up with them)
- surveying to see what really matters to them
- holding an event which brings customers together

The idea is to probe them to see what I important to them and what they would like to see improve in the future.

Reactive methods mean you get their VoC information:

- complaints or customers screaming at you.
- dashboards or metric scorecards where you can see the RED-YELLOW-GREEN.
- feedback from social media, i.e. Twitter, Facebook etc.
- website inquiries or concerns.

Ideally, you want to be proactive but, in many cases, your project will be identified by reactive feedback.

Chapter 4: Business Process Maps

Process maps show the easiest way to visualize the flow of the steps being executed. It's a great way to Capture the way of working, identify any breakdowns in the flow of operations or see waste and help teams spot opportunities for improvements. Like the saying goes, "a picture can say a thousand words!" Process maps give the team a graphical way of communicating any problems to management.

There are many types of visual process mapping tools out there including software packages. The ones we are going to high light in this book are the following types:

- High Level process where in less than 12 activities you show the flow of a process. This is used in a SIPOC (found in Chapter 5), Charter (found in Chapter 6) and/or business case. An example:

- Flowcharting is putting together process mapping steps with include diamonds as decision steps. Usually these types are used in ISO documents, PMI body of knowledge or even your company's Quality system.

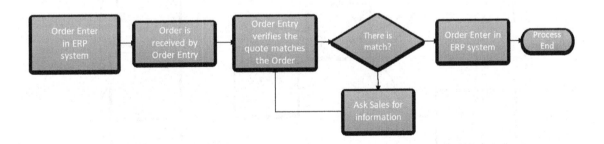

- Swim lane flowcharts takes the flowcharting to the next level by placing the step as a task boxes within the respective job titles (swim lane) so you understand who is responsible for this step.

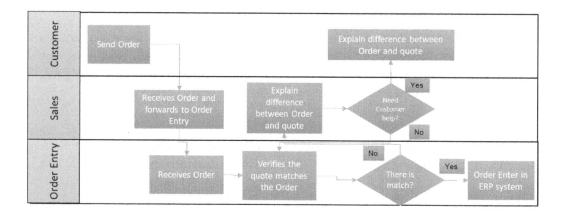

- Spaghetti or workflow diagrams (found in Chapter 18) show physical flow or work and usually describe the chaos of going back and forth in a process.

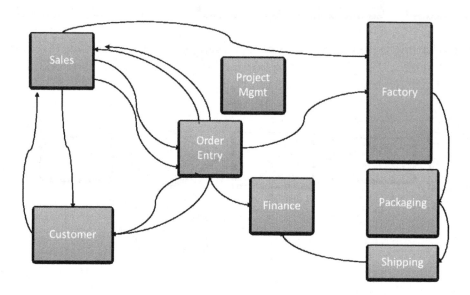

- Value Stream Mapping (VSM) (found in Chapter 19) is process mapping after you observed the process firsthand. In Lean, you "go to the Gemba" which means you go where the process is and observe firsthand the steps involved. You measure each step by time allotted. Once you completed your observations, you map out the process including the time for each step. Next, you are able to visually see what is considered to be value-add or nonvalue-add for the customer. We will go into details in a later chapter.

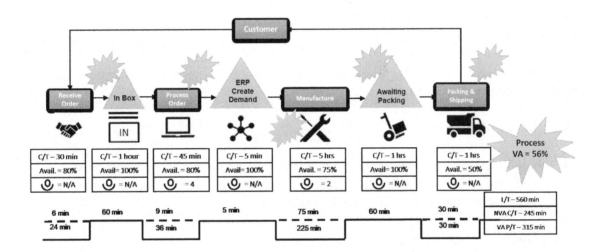

Chapter 5: SIPOC Diagram

We are going to use the SIPOC to visualize at a high level the main points of your project including:

- The inputs and outputs of the process you are trying to improve
- Who influences your inputs
- The customer receiving your output
- What data you should be looking into
- Scoping out your project.

When putting together a SIPOC, you need to make sure you can answer the questions for each step represented by a letter.

Let's go through each one:

- **S**upplier(s): who is your supplier(s) that supply you with the required inputs to satisfy the customer needs? i.e. suppliers can be internal – a function, dept or point of contact or external – a dealer, wholesaler, etc.
- **I**nput(s): what are the items or activities that you need to place through the process in order to create outputs for the customer needs?
- **P**rocess: what are the key process steps that are required to create the product or service that the customer requires?
- **O**utput(s): what is the final product or service that you give to the customer and will satisfy their CTQs
- **C**ustomer(s): who is/are receiving the product or service and have given you the requirements on the output?

When speaking to management about your project, you should be able to summarize your overview information of the project using only one slide. To view a sample SIPOC template you can use, go to Appendix B.

This tool is known as SIPOC because it looks at improving the flow of the process starting from the supplier and ending with the customer. Now, if you take the customer as your starting point, you are actually thinking of what is required to satisfy your customer's CTQs. In this case, you are looking at it as COPIS, not SIPOC and the template helps you think from a customer's perspective by have two additional questions answered: "what the customer wants?" and "does the process incorporate all the inputs?" The truth is it does not matter how you initially put this diagram together. What is important is that once you complete answering the questions for each of the sections, you are able to tell the story going one way or the other. For this reason, you see the arrows going from customer to output and from process to input.

One final note when filling in the process box. In this template you want to place 10-12 steps max to represent the high-level process you want to improve. Once we enter Measure and Analyze phases, you will be detailing out the process using a Value Stream Map.

In Appendix B, under SIPOC you will find the template along with a simple example, manufacturing a water bottle. Read the diagram from left to right or going with the flow of the process. The main supplier is the one supplying us with the purified spring water. As inputs to the manufacturing process, we will need bottles, caps, label and the water. You can see the high-level process has nine high level steps. The output is a bottle filled with water which is shipped to our customers that are the grocery stores.

Now let's look at it from another perspective, using COPIS logic which is looking at the SIPOC from right to left instead of left to right. So instead of putting the diagram together as a Supplier-Input-Process-Output-Customer (SIPOC) flow, you are starting with the Customer and flowing backwards (Customer-Output-Process-Input-Supplier) The grocery stores want bottled water that is purified and comes from a spring. In other words, the customers want clean drinking water. To give them this requirement, we need certain materials, which come from the input. Regardless whether you are reading the diagram left to right or right to left, the information placed is consistent validating your customer's CTQs are met!

Chapter 6: Project Charter

You now have a good understanding of what problem you want to solve and the process you will improve. It is time to put together your charter, so you have a document to communicate with your management. This initiates your start of your change management journey.

You are going to need a clear and concise way of depicting your project to keep the stakeholders focused. It is also your vehicle to informing management of status and ensuring their support. You want to make sure you align the project to your company's organizational objectives and clarify the expectations of the project outcome. In some case, used to authorize the project, especially if you do not have a business case. Go to Appendix B to find a sample template for the charter as well as an example filled out.

A good project charter will have the following main items:

- Clear problem statement
- A goal to decrease / increase / eliminate the defect
- Clear unit of measure (i.e. customer response)
- Clear measure of the unit (i.e. wait time)
- Can establish the Baseline (i.e. 24 to 86 hrs.)
- Can establish the Target (i.e. 8 hrs.)

Before we dive into the charter, let us take some time to understand the difference between an error and a defect.

6.1 Defect versus Error

An Error is the cause of the Defect while the Defect is the result of the Error. Have I confused you? Think of it this way. The reason or cause for you to embark on a project is due to the errors occurring now with the current process. Brainstorming what is causing the errors to occur will yield the defect(s) in your process. For example, you began this project because you have many customers complaining (this is the error). When you dug into the process, you found the defects stopping you from giving the customers what they want.

Cause

- Errors
- Mistakes
- Issues

Effects
- Defects or Process breakdowns
- Incomplete, incorrect or damaged
- Waste or non-value-added work

6.2 LSS Charter

The main components you will be addressing when you put together your charter are:

- **Business Case**: high level explanation of the "why" this project is important
- **Problem Statement:** explain "what" the issue you are trying to solve is
- **Defect Definition**: based on the problem statement, what is the defect you will be measuring?
- **Customer CTQ(s):** what are the customers' needs, expectations and/or requirements
- **Project Goal(s):** explain the objectives for this project; "what" is this project going to accomplish
- **Success Criteria:** what should happen to make this project a success?
- **IN / OUT Scope:** "IN" is what part of this project is; "OUT" what is not going to be part of the project
- **Process(es) affected**: what process or processes are affected by your project
- **Target Benefit(s):** what value(s) does this project bring; qualitative and/or quantitative savings
- **Assumption(s):** list any theories or suppositions you have on this project
- **Constraint(s):** what are the roadblocks or hurdles for this project?
- **Project Team (Name / Role / Commitment):** list out people that are going to be working on this project with you along with their role and how much they will be committing to it (in %)
- **Schedule (Baseline / Actual):** put table together with milestones, phases or stages along with the dates you intend to finish (Baseline); when the item occurs, place the actual date; Status(on track, behind, ahead, closed, not started) is sometimes included to inform stakeholders where you are at

Unless you are the luckiest person in the world, you know that a project goes through iterations during its lifespan. A charter is no different. It is a live document that gets updated as information gets clearer and/or changes occur. Since we are going to use the charter as your communication vehicle to management, it should always have the latest information. When following this book, aim to update your charter at every Phase with any new information you have. This may include schedules change, resource changes, new or revised assumptions/constraints, and benefits becoming more tangible.

Chapter 7: DICE

DICE was developed by Harold L. Sirkin, Perry Keenan and Alan Jackson in their white paper, "The Hard Side of Change Management". It is a scoring methodology to understand the health of your project. You can calculate the score at any point in your project to get a snapshot of your project's health. It is suggested, similar to the charter, to calculate your DICE score at the beginning of every phase so you are aware of how your project is progressing.

DICE stands for:

- **D**uration refers to the period between project gates or key decision checkpoints.
- **I**ntegrity refers to team's reliability in making the project successful.
- **C**ommitment is not limited to the team members (C2), but also senior management (C1).
- **E**ffort refers to the amount of time and energy the team members need for the project on top of what they already have on hand.

Equation: $D + (2 \times I) + (2 \times C1) + C2 + E = Score$

Here is the equation created which yields a score. Now let us go through each one with a little more detail to help you score effectively.

7.1 Duration

Duration looks at how long a change initiative takes, the more likely it is to go off-track. So, the questions you ask are:

- *How long will the project take to complete?*
- *For long projects, there are gates or milestones…. How long is the next major milestone?"*

Why is "*Duration*" important?

The longer a change initiative takes, the more likely it is to go off-track.

How to improve "*Duration*"?

- Reduce the time frame between the milestones
- Re-engineer the structure of the milestones…are they occurring regularly? Do they move the project to the next phase? Are stakeholders present and engaged?

7.2 Integrity

Integrity is important for LSS projects because of all the change management you need to do preparing the employees for the change to come. You need to have the right people with the right skill set be part of the team and capable of working on the project. Make sure that you have everyone understanding their place in the team as well as their responsibilities. If you, yourself require some help in the project manager position, seek it out by getting a mentor or coach:

- *Project team have the right skill set.*
- *Is everyone capable and available for the project?*

Why is "*Integrity*" important?

Having the right people make up the team and performing the tasks is an integral whole will set up the project for success. Your goal is to improve a process the right way that will be used by the people that are part of the process.

How do I improve "*Integrity*"?

- Ensure the people have sufficient technical skills
- The project leader is capable
- Everyone understands their respective roles and responsibilities on the project.

7.3 Commitment

Commitment is important when you are planning on making a paradigm shift in the organization, you need top down buy-in to the project. But top down approach alone is not going to make it a success. You also require buy-in from management and employees. Basically, all levels of your organization should have at least one promoter helping you out with change management. So, when we look at commitment, we have it split into senior management and the team you are going to form. Make sure your team has those people in the right levels to help you through the change.

- *Do you have buy-in of senior management, your sponsor and your team?*
- *Are they committed to ensure the change will occur and be part of making it happen?*

Why is "*Commitment*" important?

Top level commitment trickling down to the other levels is important for the project to succeed. Commitment of your stakeholders is important during the project planning and execution, but it is essential for implementation. You want your improved process to be adopted within your organization.

How to improve "*Commitment*"?

- C_1 Senior Management: have them demonstrate their commitment to the organization…i.e. town halls, newsletters, etc.
- C_2 PM and team: enhance communications within the team; be able to demonstrate the project's importance to senior management, i.e. quick hits.

7.4 Effort

Effort is important because you need people to spend time on the project properly so it can get done. And in today's world, resources are doing multi-jobs or stretched with other initiatives, so you are competing to get them on your project. Make sure you have a sense of what needs to happen in your project, possibly a schedule with milestones so you can explain to your team how much time as well as when they are required to jump in.

- *Does each team member have the project as part of their Goals & Objectives, standard work or mandate?*
- *you have buy-in of senior management, your sponsor and your team?*

Why is "*Effort*" important?

Just getting someone to say they will be on your team only to see that they don't have the time to do what is required of them becomes an obstacle for your project. Remember, you are competing for the resources to be on your project. Having the right resources accomplishing the required activities on your project in the time allotted is an accomplishment in itself.

How do I improve "*Effort*"?

- As project lead, manage your team resources effectively, transitioning them in / out of the project incl. even workload or incremental work

- See to have some key resources dedicated in the phase you require them, suspending their standard work or some non-core activities

7.5 DICE Tool

Go to Appendix B to view the sample DICE template looks like. Based on the score, you are able to see whether your project's health is a "Win", "Worry" or "Woe". If you are in a "Worry" or "Woe" state, you should put actions in place to get you down to a "Win" position. If you are in the "Win" state, then make sure you know what your main drivers are so that you stay in this state while you are executing on your DMAIC project.

Chapter 8: Pre-Mortem

There is a great article from Harvard Business on Pre-Mortem, but the real wakeup call is a 19 min 11 sec video by Mark Kozak-Holland, showing what really went wrong with the Titanic as lessons learned and how it could have been avoided if risk management was executed properly. Here is the link to the YouTube video: https://www.youtube.com/watch?v=wbvfir2x344

Instead of waiting to record your lessons learned or postmortem for your project, you are going to start your project by conducting a pre-mortem. You get your project team together and look at the worst-case scenario at the beginning of your project. Start with "the project failed" and brainstorm possible reasons why it failed. Make sure you're doing this with a cross functional team because there are things you will not think of which may occur. The exercise should not be more than an hour or so. Human nature is that if asked "what went wrong" you'll get a longer answer than if you ask, "what went right".

The pre-mortem exercise will tie into your FMEA or Failure Mode and Effects Analysis (found in Chapter 9). You basically get with your team, accept that the project has ended as a failure. Solicit reasons why this happened in a brainstorming session. Record all the findings, prioritizing them from best case of occurring to the least plausible.

This proactive approach helps:

- Look at the worst case Instead of waiting for the end of a project to conduct a Lessons Learned or Post-Mortem
- Capture all concerns by conducting the pre-mortem with a broad cross-functional team
- The exercise yields as outcome project risk areas to monitor and failure modes

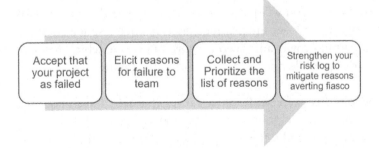

Accept that your project as failed → Elicit reasons for failure to team → Collect and Prioritize the list of reasons → Strengthen your risk log to mitigate reasons averting fiasco

Remember that an effective pre-mortem occurs at the start of your project after you have scoped out your project and have completed your charter. This ensures that you and your team are on the same page. Most of the time you, as the team lead or project manager, can facilitate the group and record all findings. But in some cases, you may want to be part of the brainstorming and get a facilitator as a 3rd party to facilitate the exercise.

Make sure the team attends this meeting. You don't want to piecemeal this exercise by conducting it one-on-one. When everyone is in a room, one idea can easily get someone else thinking of another reason. You want to have that dynamics for this exercise.
If you have issues starting off the facilitation, and the "let imagine this project failed" opener does not work, here are questions you can use as ice breakers:

- Why did we start this project? Problem statement & Goal(s)
- What is IN scope and what is OUT?
- Who will be impacted with this project?
- What are the Expectations from the customer, stakeholders and us as a team?
- How was this project being measured? Which company's Key Performance Indicators (KPI)s was it tied to and we did not meet?

Keep the meeting light, especially since most of the conversation is around a negative topic. Have fun with it and go crazy with some out of this world ideas....it usually lightens the mood. Go to Appendix B to view a sample pre-mortem template you can use. The following steps to fill the form:

- You will fill in the title box with your name, the names of your team, the project name, date and if you will have a facilitator, their name
- Next you will record all the issues coming from yourself and the team during this meeting - record them on the last column as potential failures effects.
- Now you are going to work backwards and fill in the other columns: which category or dept. the issue would fall into in the first column
- which process task, step, or if it's a factory setting, the part number is tied to each cause on the second column
- on the third column you will place cause for the issue that is occurring. For example, if the customer doesn't get the product, then it's because we ended up scraping the customized part internally and need to start a new one which will be heavy delays to the customer's schedule on site. So, the potential failure is scrap.

Do not limit yourself in this exercise. Look at causes that may have occurred with the project itself as well as anything that can go wrong at the managerial level. For example, the project manager (you) got a new job and left the dept. halfway through the project which is why it failed. You should target at least a dozen things that go wrong.

MEASURE PHASE

To understand the problem, you need to be able to measure the problem. Thus, to improve the process you have scoped, you need to be able to collect its output data.

When you go to a doctor, you tell them your symptoms. More often than not, this is not enough information to diagnose your problem. So, they send you for blood tests and that is how they collect data.

Chapter 9: Failure Mode & Effects Analysis (FMEA)

This failure mode and effect analysis tool or FMEA is one of the most famous tools in the risk realm. It is widely adopted as well as modified by many companies, creating their own spin to the tool. There is a high possibility you are already using a similar version at work. In this book, we are going to be using the one found in Appendix B which ties to the pre-mortem you completed in the last chapter.

If you recall from the pre-mortem tutorial, you already have the first four columns of the FMEA completed. Simply transfer this information into the FMEA template and start populating the other columns depending on where you with the risk.

Let us recap, the Pre-Mortem was looking at your project failing at the start so that it opens up many possibilities. This is considered the "what" piece of the FMEA. Now you are going to brainstorm with your team:

- Why this can happen?
- When does it occur?
- What is the deficiency that results in the failure mode?
- Finally, you will be placing what your current controls are today that can identify this failure. If you have no controls today, then that is a problem within itself and you would list that there are no controls.

These questions will complete the risk identification, root cause, actions and identify specific people taking these actions to decrease its likelihood of the risk from occurring.

In some cases, you will already come up with some recommended actions. In other cases, you are still at the beginning of your project and haven't figured it out. Thus, at this point, your FMEA should be answering the questions you see here as best you can. As your journey progresses, you will be able to continue updating the information, recommending actions, its owner(s) and finally, when the eventual action is taken.

Note: DO NOT fill out this entire sheet and think that your risk analysis is checked off in your project. This tool is live during the execution of your project and thus, you should be reviewing and updating it at every team meeting. There may be new risks you will add during your journey as you start closing out some of the ones you already have identified through risk mitigation. In some cases, you may have a risk specific to a phase of the framework, so when this possible failure does not materialize, and the threat has pasted, then you will be able to close it out with no required action.

The FMEA tool is also equipped with a way to prioritize the risks and highlight to your stakeholders which risks are critical to the project. This is done by measuring the following:

- Severity: which covers how significant the impact of the effect is to the customer. This looks at the potential failure effort and rates it with a number. It goes from the failure not effecting the customer to endangering the customer.
- Occurrence: which looks at how likely is the Cause of the failure mode to occur? So, it can be a one off or it's a certainty that it will occur.
- Detection: which looks at how likely will the current system detect the Cause or Failure Mode if it occurs? Basically, it can be that the occurrence of this failure goes undetected or it is easily detected.

Once you rated your severity, occurrence, and detection for a failure by using a 1(best case) to 10 (worst case) scale, the multiplication of the three scales will yield an RPN or Risk Priority Number. You will use these numbers to prioritize your failure and help you choose which one you should focus on first. As a rule of thumb, the lower the number the better.

How do you know what to place numerically? The guide I still use is taken from my General Electric Six Sigma Body of Knowledge I received over twenty years ago that best describes the different levels. Go to Appendix B to view this table.

You will notice that the severity, occurrence, detection calculating the RPN is found before and after the action is taken. This is to see if you were able to reduce the failure with the action taken and by how much. By the end of your DMAIC journey, hopefully you have mitigated all the risks identified. If some pertain to deployment and adoption of your new improved process, you will need to pass on these risks to the process owner. This is why it's important to use this tool throughout your journey and review it regularly.

Chapter 10: Data Collection

In LSS, data collection is the process of gathering information specifically tied to your Y or customer's CTQs. You are looking for the x's that will impact the Y. Once you know your x's, you require a systematic way of gathering the intel.

The equation you are focusing on is: $Y = f(x)$

When figuring out what data to collect, you should make sure the data:

- Is part of the process you are wanting to improve
- has a direct correlation with the customer's CTQ
- is relatively available or easy to access
- occurs more than once, so you don't only have limiting one-off data points but data points that are produced every time the process is executed yielding you a good data set to use.

Based on your VoC and SIPOC, you should have a good understanding of your customer's main CTQ, or "Y" and thus, are able to list what x's or problems you need to resolve so that it improves the customer's CTQ.

When collecting your data for analysis, please make sure it's not going to cost you a lot of money and it's relatively easy to collect. For example, take the sample project, "Improve Customer Responsiveness" where the main "Y" is getting a response in a timely fashion, then the x's would be looking at the types of issues the customers call in for and how long it takes us to respond. So, if the time required to close an issue is stored in a database, collecting your data is simple. But if there is no database, and this data was never collected by your company, it becomes more challenging. This is where you will need to collect it manually meaning you ask a couple of customer service representatives to give you all the email requests along with their responses. You then will take the date and time stamp to calculate the time it took to complete this request.

Unfortunately, you are doing this because there is no automated system that records the request's open and closed date calculating the cycle time of the transaction. Because it is done manually, it is likely your data set will be less than 100 data points, which in LSS is considered as discrete data. Target your data collection to be as reliable as possible. When possible, target it to be continuous which means you can get more than 100 data points. Whatever you do, do not make up numbers!

You want to collect data from the same source or sources using the one process you are investigating in this DMAIC project. And to be consistent, you want to collect the data when they are following the process. If the process is not being followed, then your data is not stable, and you cannot draw any conclusions from it. Without a process followed you risk having to redesign a process they will all follow, and this is more of a DFSS (Design for Six Sigma) project than DMAIC.

The number of data points in your data set should be plentiful. Therefore, when it comes to collecting the data to your project so you can analyze where the issues are, always consider collecting continuous data. Continuous data means that you can easily access, every time the process is followed, all recordings, usually through a database or system identifying the results of the process. For example, every time a rivet is scrapped because it does not meet the 0.05" specification, the machine will record the measurement comparing it to the specification and you can easily retrieve the measurements. But if you need to go on the factory floor, sit next to the operator and record how many rivets pass and how many fail, then this is discrete data. You are getting a snapshot of the data in the process, not being able to get data continuously regardless of the day

Another example from our sample Improve Customer Responsiveness Project would be an automated database the customer service representatives use to record every incoming call or email from the customer, including the time this request was submitted and the time it took for it to be resolved. In this situation, extracting the types of requests along with their cycle time is easy. But if no automated system exists, to get this information you may need to ask the customer service representatives to manually write down each request they get in a day and track it until they are able to close it. Then the data becomes discrete.

If you have a choice on your data source, Continuous Data is the best…. you have better accuracy and precision in your data pool.

Continuous Data:

- values can be measured with more precision since you have endless source of data points at your disposal
- come from a recording system or database holds the data
- measurement types incl.:
-
  - o bolt thickness, length, width, height, etc.
  - o cycle time
  - o scrap or rework measuring the amount occurring daily

Discrete Data:

- recording manually a point in time of the process (snapshot), i.e. a day, an hour, etc.
- measurement types incl:
    - pass/fail
    - good/bad
    - complete/incomplete
    - missing/not missing.

In some cases, you may have a defect where if you dig deeper, you may know that there are various reasons or defectives which make up this defect. For example, if you are looking at a form which has five fields to be filled out correctly, as soon as there is a field that is not filled out, it is a defect. But if you are able to know which of the five fields is never filled out correctly, then you will discover the defectives causing the defect to occur.

Let's take the Improve Customer Responsiveness Project again. If the customer service representatives write on a table every time they open and close a case for 3 days, then this is discrete data. You manually collect all the tables, synthesis the data and create a cycle time for a 3-day sample size only. If in these 3 days they didn't get many requests for a particular type of request, then your data may be skewed. Similarly, on the factory floor if the rivets that day were mostly within specification, your sample size will look better than what the problem real is!

Therefore, when you are looking at data collection, go continuous. If you are limited by manually collecting data, consider spending at least a week to do that, so your sample size is not small, and it gives you a better view of what is going on in your process.

Chapter 11: House of Quality using Quality Function Deployment (QFD)

In this chapter, we will be going through the House of Quality, also referred to as the Quality Function Deployment (QFD) or Cause & Effect matrix. Whatever you want to call it, the purpose of this tool is to decide on where you will focus on in your project in order to satisfy your customers' CTQs. To go through this tool for the first time, we will assume we are looking into one process. If you have multiple processes and need to narrow down to one you can focus on, use the CTQ drill down tree in Chapter 12.

There is a high probability you will have multiple CTQs from your VoC collection. You start feeling worried you will never meet your customer's expectations. The QFD helps sort out which of the CTQs you can tackle in your project and how you will be doing it.

To create your house of quality, you start by either creating an Excel spreadsheet or by drawing a table on paper with two columns. We start by placing the "what?" which are your customers' CTQs in the first column. Remember your formula, $Y=f(x)$. In this case, the CTQs are going to be your Y's. For example, my customer wants the product to be defect-free, packaged with spare parts, assembled and on-time. List them on the first column:

Defect-free
Packaged with spare parts
Assembled
On-time

Next you look at each one of these CTQs with your team and decide how important they are for the customer. This is because the customer may give you a laundry list of what they would love to see happen, but many times there are only a few which are critical for them. You may have a customer that believes everything is critical, but this is rare. They are as pragmatic as you are so they know you cannot fix it all in one shot. They will tell you the most important CTQs they want to see happen first.

Therefore, on the second column, you will rank the CTQs by placing a range from 1 to 5, where 1 is least important and 5 is the most important.

Defect-free	5
packaged with spare parts	2
Assembled	3
On-time	4

Now you will brainstorm with your team "how" you will address these CTQs. What are the deliverables you need to focus on in order to ensure these CTQs are tackled? These are going to be considered your x's. Note, there may be a brainstorm idea which will satisfy only one of the CTQs or a couple. Write it down. Make sure these are things you have the power to change or put in place in your project. Once you have these deliverables, create as many columns as needed and list each of the deliverables on the top of each column. In this example, the team brainstormed about a dozen possible deliverables. At the end of the exercise, they decided on the top five and wrote them on the top of each of the columns:

		Streamline factory flow	Pre-inspection	Establish std work	Buy new shipping materials	New cell before shipping
Defect-free	5					
packaged w/ spares	2					
Assembled	3					
On-time	4					

To make this QFD complete, we will tie each of the deliverables to the CTQs by asking the question "does this deliverable tackle this CTQ?" The response is either a high, medium, or low. We will quantify these designations as follows:

- High = 5
- Medium = 3
- Low = 1

For example, does the x = streamline factory flow make the product defect-free? How big of an impact will it tackle this CTQ, Y = Defect-free? Truthfully, if we get our process step time with respect to the customer's request under control, also known as the takt time (found in Chapter 19.1) and every step of the flow is done properly, there's a good chance we get no defects in the product. So, we will consider it high or 5. Next, does the x = streamline factory flow make the Y=packaged with spare parts happen? Not really, we can get the flow working correctly but still not package the spares at shipping. Therefore, we place a Low or 1. As so we go through each of the deliverables asking the same question, how it impacts the Y and get the following table:

		Streamline factory flow	Pre-inspection	Establish std work	Buy new shipping materials	New cell before shipping
Defect-free	5	5	5	3	1	5
packaged w/ spares	2	1	1	5	5	3
Assembled	3	3	1	5	5	5
On-time	4	3	3	5	3	3

Keep in mind when you go through the High-Med-Low discussion with your team it will be highly subjective. So, make sure you have examples to back your reasoning. The final step to creating your QFD is to total up the numbers. Let us start by adding a column and row to the table:

		Streamline factory flow	Pre-inspection	Establish std work	Buy new shipping materials	New cell before shipping
Defect-free	5	5	5	3	1	5
packaged w/ spares	2	1	1	5	5	3
Assembled	3	3	1	5	5	5
On-time	4	3	3	5	3	3

To calculate the CTQs: You multiply the CTQ's priority with each of the deliverables' number to equalize the matrix and repopulate:

		Streamline factory flow	Pre-inspection	Establish std work	Buy new shipping materials	New cell before shipping
Defect-free	5	25	25	15	5	25
packaged w/ spares	2	2	2	10	10	6
Assembled	3	9	3	15	15	15
On-time	4	12	12	20	12	12

The final step is to sum up by row and column:

		Streamline factory flow	Pre-inspection	Establish std work	Buy new shipping materials	New cell before shipping	
Defect-free	5	25	25	15	5	25	95
packaged w/ spares	2	2	2	10	10	6	30
Assembled	3	9	3	15	15	15	57
On-time	4	12	12	20	12	12	68
		48	42	60	42	58	

Now we are going to understand the results of our exercise. The greatest CTQ sum is the "defect-free". And the top scores for the x's that make up this CTQ's score are streamline factory flow, pre-inspection, and new cell before shipping. This means that we need to focus on these three deliverables if we want to satisfy this CTQ.

Let us take a different look at the results. If we look at the greatest deliverable sum, it's "establish standard work". If we focus on only this deliverable, we are able to actually impact three CTQs: packaged spare parts, assemble and on-time.

So, where do we go from here? Well, it all depends on what you want to accomplish in this project. If we decide we want to tackle the two top CTQs from the customer: defect-free and on-time, then we will look at which deliverables are important to focus on to make this happen. In this case, the x's are going to be:

- streamline factory flow,

- pre-inspection,
- new cell before shipping,
- establish standard work.

Let us look at the steps we just went through:

- Step 1: List Customer CTQs…what does my customer want?
- Step 2: Prioritize the Customer CTQs…what does my customer deem critical?
- Step 3: Brainstorm and list the deliverables…how will we satisfy these CTQs?
- Step 4: Complete the House of Quality by placing H - 5, M - 3, L – 1 by asking the question "does this deliverable tackle this CTQ?"
- Step 5: Calculate the relationship between the X's and the Y's by multiplying the CTQs' priority number with the H, M, L designation.
- Step 6: Calculate the sums for each CTQ and each deliverable
- Step 7: Understanding the results

We are going to go through another example, the "Improve Customer Responsiveness" project, to ensure you understand the steps:

- Step 1: List Customer CTQs…what does my customer want?

  - Quick response
  - Person answering
  - Quick call back (or read receipt)
  - On-time delivery

- Step 2: Prioritize the Customer CTQs… what does my customer deem critical?

  - Quick response -- 5
  - Person answering -- 3
  - Quick call back (or read receipt) -- 4
  - On-time delivery -- 2

- Step 3: Brainstorm and list the deliverables…how will we satisfy these CTQs?

  - Request Cycle time - CT [from open to closing the request]
  - Available hours [currently 8AM-5PM]
  - Callback Cycle time - CT [start time when customer contacts to when we contact back]

- Delivery Cycle time - CT [left the warehouse & arrives on customer site]
- Customer Service
- Technical Representative
- Warehouse Representative

- Step 4: Complete the House of Quality by placing H - 5, M - 3, L – 1 by asking the question "does this deliverable tackle this CTQ?"

		Request CT	Available hours	Callback CT	Delivery CT	Customer Service	Tech Rep.	Warehouse
Quick response	5	5	5	5	1	5	3	3
Person answering	3	5	5	3	1	5	1	1
Quick call back	4	3	5	5	1	5	1	1
On-time delivery	2	1	1	1	5	3	1	5

- Step 5: Calculate the relationship between the X's and the Y's by multiplying the CTQs' priority number with the H, M, L designation.

		Request CT	Available hours	Callback CT	Delivery CT	Customer Service	Tech Rep.	Warehouse
Quick response	5	25	25	25	5	25	15	15
Person answering	3	15	15	9	3	15	3	3
Quick call back	4	12	20	20	4	20	4	4
On-time delivery	2	2	2	2	10	6	2	10

- Step 6: Calculate the sums for each CTQ and each deliverable

		Request CT	Available hours	Callback CT	Delivery CT	Customer Service	Tech Rep.	Ware house	
Quick response	5	25	25	25	5	25	15	15	135
Person answering	3	15	15	9	3	15	3	3	63
Quick call back	4	12	20	20	4	20	4	4	84
On-time delivery	2	2	2	2	10	6	2	10	34
		54	62	56	22	66	24	32	

- Step 7: Understanding the results

  - Top Y Score – CTQ: Quick Response; to impact this CTQ, we need to focus on these following x's:

    - Request Cycle time - CT [from open to closing the request]
    - Available hours [currently 8AM-5PM]
    - Callback Cycle time - CT [start time when customer contacts to when we contact back]
    - Customer Service

  - Top x Score – deliverable: Customer Service; if we focus on this deliverable in our project, we are going to be impacting the following CTQs:

    - Quick response
    - Person answering
    - Quick call back (or read receipt)

As a conclusion to this second example, we are going to look at the following Y = F(x):
Quick Response = f (Customer Service, Available hours, Request CT, Callback CT)

Keep in mind we are using the House of Quality only at the first level. For more complex problems, the QFD can actually have houses of quality, not just one. We are not going to go into this topic for this book.

Chapter 12: CTQ Drill Down Tree

Most of you know what process you are going to be looking at. In fact, through the SIPOC diagram, you actually mapped out your high-level process. But let's say you are unsure, or worse, you believe you need to address multiple processes.

This tool will either confirm that you are on the right track, show you that you forgot some other processes that should be looked into, or give you a completely different process than the one you placed in your SIPOC. This tool is used when you want to tie the customers' CTQs to your internal processes which you control. Go to Appendix B to view a sample template for the drill down tree. This tool will turn your customer CTQs into project CTQs, similar to the QFD but it does not look into the project x's. It will only reveal to you what process or processes impact your customer's CTQ(s). To create your drill down tree:

1. You start at the top by deciding if your project is looking at a product or a service as its outcome. If you are looking at delivering a component or paperwork to your customer, it's a product. If you are going to be repairing a machine or answer customer questions, then it is a service.
2. Next list the sub-products or services. For example, if delivering to the customer, a component which is made up of three parts, then list each part as a sub-product. If we take the example of repairing a machine, which include the steps of running a diagnostic, fixing the errors and commissioning machine for use. In this case I have three sub-services.
3. Now that you identified the product or service as well as its next level of detail, we start listing the customer CTQs right below and tying them to the sub-product or sub-service. The idea is to tie the CTQ to the sub-product or sub-service it will best correlate to. You may have a CTQ that shares more than one sub-product or sub-service, do not fret, this is normal.
4. List the possible processes you believe these sub-products or sub-services follow. These processes are what you control, and you believe are required to be looked at in your process.
5. Lastly you will draw an arrow from the CTQ to the process you believe it correlates to (or will impact).

Keep in mind, when you collect your VoC, you will get from your customer(s) one to a couple of requirements, rarely more than five. Take the Improve Customer Responsiveness Project as an example and go see in Appendix B to see how it can be is laid out as either by looking at it as a product or as a service.

A. As a Service:

    a. the drill down tree is depicting customer service given to all customers that buy the company's products.

    b. How can the customer reach a representative? By email or phone. So, these are my 2 sub-services.

    c. For the emails, what was my voice of the customer requirements? They wanted to have a read receipt, so they know when someone looks at their request and of course, a quick response.

    d. Similarly, if they called in, they wanted to talk to a person, not a recording and get quick response or call back if the rep could not answer their question while on the phone.

    e. All these CTQs are really tied to one process, the customer service process. So basically, I can look into the customer CTQs by simply looking into one internal process.

B. As a Product:

    a. The drill down tree is depicting the type of requests coming in as a product. Basically, we are looking at the requests instead of the responsiveness.

    b. In this case there are 5 main request types that come in: deliver, order status, product information, incomplete orders and damaged goods.

    c. The customer CTQs don't change and are the getting the request answered quickly, talking to a person, and read receipt from their emails. Furthermore, there are request types specifically for damaged goods where the customer's CTQ is to get their replacement parts quickly and for delivery information they want to hear that their product has shipped.

    d. When looking internally to see which processes these types of requests follow, you see we have more than just the customer service process listed.

    e. Drawing the arrows from the CTQ to the process it impacts will complete the drill down tree exercise. To select the process, you will go into detail in your journey, you count which process tackles the majority of the CTQs. In this case, the process is still the customer service one.

Chapter 13: Test Retest Study

You perform the Test-Retest study before conducting a Gage R&R study, also known as the Gage Repeatability and Reproducibility Study (found in the next Chapter) so to understand your data source. It reveals your Measurement System Analysis' (MSA) accuracy and/or precision. What it looks at is the error in the repeatability and the precision of your measurement. As a minimum, you require 10 to 15 data points to run the study. Keep in mind, as always, the more data points you have, the more reliable your results will be. Minitab® will be the choice of software to use for this method. The calculation will yield the Mean and the Standard Deviation of your MSA.

- Precise:
  - Imagine a dart board where all of the darts are off from the bullseye but close together. i.e. you keep throwing the darts off to the right
  - then you are always hitting the same place, just not the target
  - if you run Minitab® to see your bell curve visually, you'll find that it is displaying a problem with centering, which means your curve is going to look skewed or off the target
  - this off target is measured by measuring standard deviation (StDev)

- Accurate:
  - Imagine a dart board where all of the darts are everywhere, some hitting the bullseye but many others all around. i.e. you keep throwing the darts on a different spot on the board
  - Therefore, it's luck you hit the target, most of the time you are missing it and the darts are randomly spread out
  - if you run Minitab® to see your bell curve visually, you'll find that it is displaying a problem with spread, which means your curve is going to look wide with your target being somewhere in the spread
  - this widespread is measured by measuring the Mean

For your project, the target can be either precise, accurate, or both. In other words, you are looking to see whether you are off target or within the target range with high variability. Ideally, you want to be precise and accurate by the end of your project. We start by collecting our data points. If possible, collect data points from multiple operators or equipment because it helps you prepare for your Gage R&R in the next chapter. The idea is to take the data you plan to use for all your stats and run it through the test retest study first to see how reliable it is. Take the Improve Customer Responsiveness project as the example. We will look at the cycle time of our response from two customer service representatives.

13.1 Process Precision

Since precision is measured by standard deviation, the best report to run using the Minitab® software is the Descriptive Statistics report. Go to Appendix A for the step-by-step instructions to conduct this report which yields:

- Visually, a graph displaying the bell curve with bars and box plot:

    o Remember, if you have a wide bell curve, then you are NOT ACCURATE; if your bell curve is off your desired target, then you are NOT PRECISE.
    o Similarly, if you are looking at the bars, you can see how many repeatable data points landed together
    o Box plot: Imagine if you were looking at the bell curve from above, the lines in the plot is the curve. This gives you another view on how widespread your data is, and any asterisks are outliers or one-offs. Think of it as you are throwing the darts, then your friend talks to you right at the moment you throw, and it misses the board completely. They are skewing your statistical results, so ideally you want to remove those points and rerun the report before proceeding. Remember to root cause any outliers you decide to remove to make sure it's not a normal occurrence when you pull from your data source.

- Statistics: looking at the right side of the report:

    o P-value: your data is normally distributed when the p-value > 0.05
    o Mean: will tell you that on average where most of your data points landed
    o Standard Deviation (StDev): will tell you how off you are from your target and how much variation you have in your process.
    o Variance: will give you the width of your bell curve looking at the smallest and biggest data points.

To calculate exactly how off you are from your target, you will use this formula:

- StDev < 1/10 x tolerance

This report gives you the StDev number. You need to decide what your desired target is and how far you would be fine with being. In other words, what is your ideal tolerance? Let us take the Improve Customer Responsiveness Project as an example, our target is to get back to the customer within 8 hours or less and running the descriptive statistics report gave us a 6.603 for our StDev. Our range or tolerance is 8 minus 0, or 8. Now if we place the numbers in the formula we get:

- 6.603 > 0.8 where StDev is bigger than one tenth of our tolerance.

Now we know that ideally, we want to be less than 8 hours because our business hours are nine to five and not 24/7. Therefore, if we tell the customers that chances are, we will get back to them within 2 days, the range becomes 0 to 16 instead of 0 to 8, giving us a tolerance of 16. Regardless if we redo the calculation, we will find that the StDev is still bigger, so this process is NOT PRECISE.

13.2 Process Accuracy

To look at the accuracy of your data, we look at the Mean of your process. We can simply use the descriptive statistics report we just ran. However, I prefer running control charts for accuracy because if you recall from the dartboard example, this tells us how close we are to the target when we keep hitting the board at different spots. If you use control charts, you also get to see if your process is in or out of control.

If your data points come from multiple operators or equipment, then best report to run using the Minitab® software is the X-bar chart. Go to Appendix A for the step-by-step instructions to conduct this report which yields:

- Visually: a line graph between two red lines, which are the control limits. Minitab® software is great because it will highlight in red any data point, which is out of control. Nevertheless, if you go to chapters 34 and 36 you will learn more on control charting including the guidelines for observing out of control processes.
- Statistics: look at the green line in the middle that is marked as a capital "X" with a line on the top. This is the symbol for Mean in Minitab®. The number next to it is the Mean.

Do a sanity check, look at the descriptive statistics report you just ran to see if the X-bar Mean is the same number as the report's Mean. It should be. Therefore, if you find that there is a difference, go look at your data points to ensure it is the same for both tests.

Next look at your X-bar chart to see if it is in control. If you see a red point(s) or it mimics one of the eight guidelines for being out of control (see charter 34), then you know that your data is not sound. This means that regardless what you get as an accuracy calculation, if you pull the data later, your results will not be the same.

Once you have done these two checks, then we look at accuracy. To calculate exactly how accurate your process is from your Mean, you will use this formula:

- X-bar Mean – "true value"

Where you are estimating your "true value" of the test unit. Thus, if you use a "Standard Unit" or have a customer specification to uphold. Think of this as your bullseye, or your desired value that you want to achieve in your project. In our example, the target of being less than 8 hours is a standard we are aiming to respect by the end of the project. In this case, the "true value" is our desired target. Therefore, if the X-bar Mean yielded 10.45 and we desire 8 hours or less, then the calculation is:

- $10.45 - 8 = 2.45$

As a rule of thumb, you can accept the accuracy if it is less than 30% of your "true value" and the control chart shows your process in control. In this example, it is ~23% so this process IS ACCURATE.

If you were unable to get data from two operators or equipment sources, then you can still run a control chart in Minitab®, it is the I-Bar chart. Go to Appendix A for the step-by-step instructions to conduct this report. Once you ran the chart in Minitab®, follow the same steps starting from the sanity check.

Chapter 14: Gage R&R Study

This study is used to validate your measurement system. This is important because you will be using this data source in the Analyze phase to understand variation in your process. A failed Gage R&R will lead to misdiagnosing your variation, which in turn will give you false information that you will act upon in the Improve and Control phases.

We will start this chapter by recapping the types of data. It's important to know what your data is so you know which report to use in Minitab®. The mantra for LSS is always trying to get continuous data. If you are not able to, then you will have discrete data.

Continuous Data:

- values can be measured with more precision since you have endless source of data points at your disposal
- come from a recording system or database holds the data
- measurement types incl.:
    - bolt thickness, length, width, height, etc.
    - cycle time
    - scrap or rework measuring the amount occurring daily

Discrete Data:

- recording manually a point in time of the process (snapshot), i.e. a day, an hour, etc.
- measurement types incl:
    - pass/fail
    - good/bad
    - complete/incomplete
    - missing/not missing.

You will need to organize your data collection to include a minimum of two operators or equipment. The reason being you want to see if different people or machines can reproduce the process. Any differences in following the exact same process is considered variation across operators/equipment.

You will also require at least a dozen data points for each of the operators or equipment run in order to check on the repeatability. Since we are testing for repeatability, the exact sample elements should be measured by the operators/equipment at least a couple of times so you will see if there is any variation within the operator/equipment.

Let us take the Improve Customer Responsiveness project as an example. For reproducibility, we are going to select two Customer Service Representatives responding to the same time of customer request. For repeatability, we will want each of the Customer Service Representatives to respond to the same type of request twice. Thus, we plan to have five different types of requests coming in.

If we look at a factory example, we can take two lathes that are set up to cut a stainless-steel tube the exact way. We will be giving the machines four different tube lengths to cut, each of the four will be repeated once more and measure the final product's diameters to see if they are within the tolerance we specified. Set up the table with your data showing the different combinations.

Based on your data type, you will go to the correct sub-section of this chapter in order to conduct you Gage R&R study:

- Continuous Data will use Gage R&R Study – Crossed Type
- Discrete Data will use Gage R&R Study – Attribute Agreement Analysis

Both methods will reveal if your MSA is acceptable and you can proceed to the Analyze phase.

14.1 Gage R&R Study (Crossed type)

The gage R&R study is conducted to see if there is any variation in your measuring system. Ideally, you want to see the variation within the process only. We call this the part-to-part variation or actual variation.

This means you want to remove as much as possible the noise which is the variation when the operators/equipment who repeat the process is off or differences across the operators/equipment that use the same process. Unfortunately, there is always some noise in the process, which is called measurement system error or MS error.

- The MS error is made up of two variations:
  - Equipment variation (Repeatability): one or more elements
  - Appraiser variation (Reproducibility): going across

Equipment variation is when variation is found within the measurement process from one or more elements. i.e. operators have variation, or the part tolerance. Appraiser variation is when the variation goes across the measurement process. i.e. different people on your team will collect the data or will synthesize the data differently. The goal of this study is to determine if the MS error is minimum and the variation you observed is all in your process.

14.1.1 Crossed Type Gage R&R Rules

Remember the three forms of variation within your process: reproducibility, repeatability, and part-to-part variation, the next question is "how much is permitted?" Here are the rules to follow when interpreting your results for a Crossed type Gage R&R Study:

- Accept your MSA if the MS Error is less than 10%
- Decide whether you want to move forward or go back to scrub your data when your MS Error is between 10% and 30%
- Not Acceptable when the MS Error is greater than 30%. You need to figure out why there is so much of a difference in the results. Either look at getting another measurement method or root cause to find the outliers in your data source. If you can remove the outliers from your data source, then do so by scrubbing your measurement method. Then pull new data and rerun this study.
- Part-to-Part variation needs to be less or equal to 50% for effective MSA, meaning most of the variation is within the part-to-part and going on into the Analyze phase you can statistically figure out how to tackle this variation and reduce it.[7]

In Minitab®, besides the variation results, you also have the "Number of distinct categories" as a result. This is the number of groups your measurement tool can distinguish from your data. The goal is the higher the distinct categories number is, the better so that the tool is discerning one part from another. As a rule of thumb:

- 2 distinct categories, everything looks the same, your data is divided into two groups, i.e. high and low
- 3 distinct categories groups have your data divided into 3 distinct groups, i.e. low, medium, and high.
- 4 or greater distinct categories ensures your MSA is acceptable because your data has multiple distinct groups within

Let us take the Improve Customer Responsiveness project to conduct this study. The data sample would look something like this:

Request types	Customer Service Rep.	CT (hours)
Incomplete order	Lisa	13
Order Status	Lisa	11
Product Information	Lisa	5
Damaged Product	Lisa	16
Product Delivery	Lisa	8
Incomplete order	Lisa	12
Order Status	Lisa	9
Product Information	Lisa	4
Damaged Product	Lisa	15
Product Delivery	Lisa	8
Incomplete order	Lisa	11
Order Status	Anna	9
Product Information	Anna	5
Damaged Product	Anna	15
Product Delivery	Anna	7
Incomplete order	Anna	12
Order Status	Anna	10
Product Information	Anna	4
Damaged Product	Anna	16
Product Delivery	Anna	8

Go to Appendix A for the Minitab® step-by-step instructions to conduct this report which yields the following.

Graphical results using Minitab®:

- The top left-hand bar chart which will quickly tell you where the variation falls for your process (i.e. repeatable, reproducible or part-to-part). If the bars are the tallest in the part-to-part, then you are in good shape. If not, you need to see how bad the situation really is with the analytical results. Before we go there, let us finish looking at what else the graphical view will provide.
- Below the box plot shows each operator's range when handling the part also known as the R-Chart.
- Below the R-Chart is the X-bar for each operator. You recall the control charts guidelines; both the R chart and the X bar chart should show the process in control.

On the right-hand side of these three graphs shows you:

- The response for each part including the repetitions. Logic tells you that if the dots are far apart you will have a repeatable issue. Ideally, you want then to close together, possibly overlapping so you know that every measurement was the same for the same part.
- Below bar graph gives you the Mean for each of the operators. This is showing you the reproducibility, so you want to have the two Means as equal to each other as possible. Also, the boxes to be similar. If the Means are off or there are differences in the boxes, then you are looking at the operators not measuring the part the same way.
- The last graph below is the part by operator interaction. Here you will see two linear graphs with the part being on the x-axis. If the two linear lines overlap, then it's telling you that there is minimal noise in your data source. If the linear lines are apart, then you need to zoom into the part which is different and root cause why. In some cases, you may have one part being different and you can consider it an outlier, remove it from your data source and rerun this report to minimize the noise variation. However, if you do so, you need to understand why you got this noise to start with.

When you look at the analytical results, it will give you the total gage R&R % study variation (%SV) where you apply the rules we spoke at the beginning of this section. Remember you are targeting to have 10% or less, but if you don't then go for less than 30% as a minimum. Similarly, it gives you the number of distinct categories which is the measurement system's ability to detect the different characteristics. This number is the non-overlapping confidence intervals of the process variation. The more the better.

14.2 Attribute Agreement Analysis

When you have discrete data, you are using the Attribute Agreement Analysis to see if there is any variation in your measuring system. Unfortunately, chances are you are also manually collecting your data to conduct this study. Ideally, you want to get your MSA acceptable for the Analyze phase because you are going to be using this data source for conducting your capability analysis as well as your hypothesis testing.

To facilitate your data collection, start by identifying the number of operators/equipment you will be have run the process so you can collect the data. Next you need to decide on the sample parts which should be representing your entire variation range. This means that if you are looking at various screws, then select 10 different types of screws that are going to be measured by the operators to see if they pass/fail. Since we are testing for repeatability, the sample parts you select should be measured by the operators at least a couple of times so you will see if there is any variation within the operator. In addition, you require to have a standard in order to run the Attribute Agreement Analysis. A standard is the ideal outcome. For example, if the screws are looking at pass/fail data, the standard is "pass".

The Attribute Agreement Analysis measures at variation which can be repeatability, reproducibility or from the standard:

- the percentage agreement with the operator (repeatability)
- the percentage agreement between operators (reproducibility)
- the percentage agreement with the standard

Let us use the Improve Customer Responsiveness project, where we will have two customers service representatives responding to five different types of customer requests a couple of times. As long as they respond back in eight hours or less, then we consider it a "pass", if not a "fail". Our standard will be "pass".

Request types	Customer Service Rep.	Completed <8 hrs.?	Standard
Incomplete order	Lisa	Fail	Pass
Order Status	Lisa	Fail	Pass
Product Information	Lisa	Pass	Pass
Damaged Product	Lisa	Fail	Pass
Product Delivery	Lisa	Pass	Pass
Incomplete order	Lisa	Fail	Pass
Order Status	Lisa	Fail	Pass
Product Information	Lisa	Pass	Pass
Damaged Product	Lisa	Fail	Pass
Product Delivery	Lisa	Pass	Pass
Incomplete order	Lisa	Fail	Pass
Order Status	Anna	Pass	Pass
Product Information	Anna	Pass	Pass
Damaged Product	Anna	Fail	Pass
Product Delivery	Anna	Pass	Pass
Incomplete order	Anna	Fail	Pass
Order Status	Anna	Pass	Pass
Product Information	Anna	Pass	Pass
Damaged Product	Anna	Fail	Pass
Product Delivery	Anna	Fail	Pass

When you run this data through Minitab® using the Attribute Agreement Analysis, you will interpret your results. Go to Appendix A for the step-by-step instructions to conduct this report. Start with the Graphical view:

- Within Appraisers shows a line for each appraiser (operator) representing their confidence level. The closer they are to the 100%, the better because it tells you they are doing the work identically or reproducibility. The shorter the lines are, the closer each appraiser is in measuring the same part the same way or repeatability.
- Appraisers vs Standard will show you how close you are to your target or standard you supplied. Once again, you are looking for as high as possible of a percentage, ideally, 100%.

If you are good on the "Within Appraiser" graph, but you are not aligned with the standard, well you are at the right place. You need to remove that variation to improve your project. If you show variation in both, then you need to first understand where the "within appraiser" variation is coming from because it is the noise variation of your process and clean it up before looking at meeting a target. Chances are that your analytical results will tell you that you are in trouble with your measurement system. The Analytical stats results:

- Just in case you did not regard the graphical view and came straight here for the stats, the "Assessment Appraiser" will give you the percentage within appraisers and against the standard. Both should be greater than 90% for the measurement system to be accepted.
- The "Fleiss' Kappa Statistics" will give you your Kappa value of one or less. The rule of thumb is:
  - 0.9 – 1 Excellent
  - 0.7 – 0.89 Good
  - 0.5 - 0.69 Need Improvement
  - Less than 0.5, your MSA is in trouble

Kappa measures how reliable your agreement is statistical. If you do not pass, go back to your data source. Chances are you are trying to be aggressive in your target and where you are now it's just not possible so you should change it and rerun this report. For example, when we ran this report for the Improve Customer Responsiveness Project, initially we targeted 8 hours or less. But after we found our Kappa to be less than 0.5, we went back and made it less than 16 hours (or two days instead of one). This gave use the Kappa value we needed to move to the Analyze phase.

14.3 Variability in MSA

Variation in your MSA can be due to certain factors. Let us go through the main factors:

- Human error can occur when the people are not trained, or there is no work instruction / standard work for them to rely on. It can also be they are working overtime and are tired so defects escape.
- Equipment variability is when the machine you are looking at is misalignment or not calibrated properly. There are no regular inspections to ensure the equipment is up to par. In some cases, you may want to take the data at the start of the factory and the machine is not warmed up, so it is working at 60% availability.
- Environment variability is all about the area around the workplace you wish to collect data from. For example, if it is too cold, the customer service representatives will be putting on their coats and gloves so using the keyboard may be a challenge. Or look at the other extreme where it's too hot, with no air conditioning, they will be taking more breaks getting water or walking to another area where they can cool off. You want to make sure you are collecting data in a stable climate with stable conditions.
- Measurement variability may be as simple as not having the right tool to measure. The classic example is taking a ruler and measuring a screw. You may measure at the cm level or i.e. 11.43. However, if you use a digital caliper, then the screw's measurement will be at the mm or micrometer revealing 11.4368. With a ruler, you would need to estimate to get to the same level and that creates variability.
- Material variability is about collecting data where the material is of different types. So, if we keep with the ruler example, measuring an item that is flat is easier than measuring items that are slanted or rounded.
- Method variability is about how you go about to do the work. Therefore, if there are not any work instructions and all five of the people are doing it differently, this is considered an ad-hoc process. Your variability will be higher than if the five people did follow a clear instruction.

Chapter 15: Performance Standards

In this chapter, we are going to go through the basics of how Six Sigma looks at problems statistically. You recall the famous equation used is $Y=f(x)$. In fact, based on the QFD, you should have your first pass of $Y=f(x)$ formula with your CTQs and deliverables.

Let us go back to basics and understand exactly what $Y=f(x)$ entails.

- The Y being your dependent variable, is considered
    - the Symptom, which is why you, are doing this project,
    - the Output as you have identified in your SIPOC,
    - and finally known as the Effect, the "What", or "what impacts the customer?" from your QFD

- The x's are the independent variables, which consider
    - the problem or problems that exist creating the symptom,
    - the inputs and process of your SIPOC,
    - and the causes, or "the how? when? where?" from your FMEA and QFD

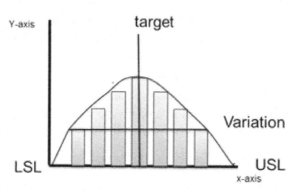

In Six Sigma philosophy, the bell curve is how you view variation in the process. The wider it is, the more variation. The more off centered from your ideal target it is, the more variation.

We map out the bell curve; it looks similar to a bell. Its center is considered the target and at both ends, you have the specification limits. The space between the is the variation.

Remember, the characteristic of the shape shows the variation, which is what customers are feeling. For example, if we are looking at cycle time with an 8 hours target. Yet the same customer may have gotten one response back in 14 hours and another in 3 hours. Therefore, the variation in the dependent variable or Y-axis is determined by the variation of each of the possible x's or independent variable.

So, what are the possible bell curves you may get in your project?

1. You can find that your process is off target. If we take the example of wanting to respond to customers within 8 hours, then ideally our Mean or true value should be 4 hours. But when we collect data, we find that the time to respond back varies from 0 (less than an hour) to 16 hours, then the true value is 8 hours. This causes an off centering from 4 to 8 hours and reveals a worse variation.
2. Maybe you collected the data and your project pretty close to your true value. Yet, the specification limits are wider apart at 0 to 24 hours. This will give you a wide bell curve where the variation is high. Take the above example, the customer feels this excessive variation. They may call in regularly to get information on their orders and they find that sometimes the response is within minutes, other times it takes a day, two or three.

If you recall from the Test Retest Study chapter, another way of thinking of these two types of variation is by looking at then as precision and accuracy.

- Precise: is when you are off target or using the earlier example, you are always hitting the same place on the dartboard, just not the bullseye.

- Accurate: is when you are hitting all around the bullseye, maybe you even got the bullseye a couple of times but most of your darts are widespread out on the dartboard.

Remember, ideally you want to be accurate and precise with your process data.

The definition of performance standard is a requirement, specification, or prerequisite enforced by the Customer through the CTQs

You are actually trying to answer questions like: "what does my customer care about?" "what is the defect(s)?" "what do I measure in the process?"

The aim of the performance standard is to translate the customer's need(s) to measurable characteristics where you start with the customer's need, listing the main CTQs and drill down into its characteristics, measure, target and spec's limits.

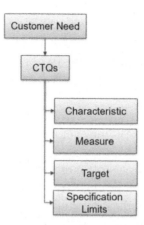

Let us look at the "Improve Customer Responsiveness" project:

- The main CTQ found by running the CTQ drill down tree and QFD is "Quick Response".
- The characteristic will be looking at the cycle time of these requests.
- What will be measured is the time the customer calls in and the request is open to when the customer is answered, and the request is closed.
- The target is to do this within 8hrs or less but if we recall the bell curve, this will put me at an ideal target of 4 hrs.
- Finally, the specification limits are within 1 business day. Since we have our offices opened for 8 hrs. a day, the lower limit to be quick turnaround, an open and close case, so zero while the upper limit will be 8 hrs.

Therefore, for this project example, the performance standard would look like this:

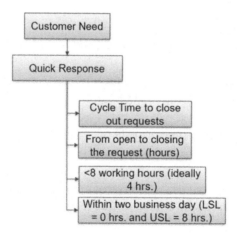

Chapter 16: Introduction to Lean

The Lean philosophy is all about the customer. It is best described by the Five-Step Thought Process Proposed by Womack & Jones in 1996 to guide managers through a Lean Transformation which is the following:

1. Specify **VALUE** from the standpoint of the **End Customer**
2. Identify all the steps in the **Value Stream**, eliminating whenever possible those steps that do not create value to the **End Customer**
3. Make the value-creating steps occur in tight sequences to flow smoothly towards the **End Customer**
4. Let the **End Customer** pull value from the upstream activity
5. As value is specified, value streams are identified, wasted steps are removed and flow w/pull are introduced. Continuous Improvement striving towards perfect value with no waste for **End Customer**.

Therefore, what you should take away from this is:

- *LEAN* is all about the *PEOPLE* performing *PROCESSES* with the aid of *TOOLS* in order to align to the *Company's Strategy* and satisfy the *Customers' Requirements.*

In a traditional non-lean company, chances are that improvements are performed sporadically and only in reactive mode: fix it once it is broken. Furthermore, this type of company may have pockets of groups doing continuous improvement, but not everyone is aligned or knowledgeable. Therefore, what occurs is that you get one department improving because they decided no longer to do some tasks, which are thrown over the fence to another department who is vaguely aware they just got more tasks to accomplish in their daily work. Take for example, a global company, let's call it XYZ. This company has a subsidiary in Italy that follows local standards, same in Panama while the US and Canada subsidiaries have consolidated processes. In lean philosophy, XYZ has no standardization because there is no one way of working regardless of location. Think about it, if Panama comes up with an efficient way of processing orders, the other subsidiaries won't benefit from it. Panama can communicate through a newsletter or present in a leadership forum. But at the end of the day, other subsidiaries can choose to stay complicit to their ways or adopt the change. What makes it more convoluted is if the XYZ employees who came up with the improvements in Panama leave or are promoted to a new role. Do their replacements adopt the change or go back to the old ways? In some cases, the improvement lives on but unfortunately, most of the time the improvement is not standardized correctly, and the new employees adopt their own way of working. Transfer of intellectual information is lost within the company. Because of all these possibilities occurring, when we think of a non-Lean company, we think of a zigzag or choppy way of continuous improvement. The effectiveness of the improvement as well as its adoption is not high. A great example is when a value employee leaves an organization and next thing you know you see two or three people taking over this employee's tasks. Basically, this employee improved their way of working to be effective but either failed to communicate the improvements or was shutout by their management.

In the Lean world, all intellectual information is retained, documented, and used to train employees. A standard is in place, which makes it easier to apply continuous improvement. Remember, to apply continuous Improvement, there needs to be a starting point, i.e. a current process everyone follows. If everyone is working ad-hoc, then there is no standard and thus, the company needs to think of establishing one before they can get into rhythm of continuous improvement. A lean company will have employees at every level questioning the status quo, embracing change and empowered them to improve their way of working continuously. Once the improvement is achieved, it is documented, and training is performed. If you imagine a graph now, you will see an upwards line without any zigzags.

Traditionally, a company believed that to reach high quality, the internal costs needed to increase…. basically, it costs more to have high quality, or it costs more to be on time with deliveries. However, Lean looks at how to reduce waste internally so that you lower the costs, improve the quality, and are always meeting the customer demand.

Final comparison between a traditional company and a Lean company is how they think of value-added work. Lean thinks of value added being what the customer would pay for. Any other task performed for internal use is found to be a waste because you are not getting money from the customer in order to accomplish this task. In a traditional company all tasks are considered value-added making it harder to find improvements until something crashes. Therefore, unlike a Lean company, a traditional one usually ends up improving on value-added (VA) tasks and ignoring the real underlining non-value added (NVA) ones.

In Lean, there are three types of Wastes or non-value-added tasks:

1. **MURA** is the Japanese term meaning unevenness: Have you ever had a job where you have quiet days and then you have crazy long days? Unevenness is a problem in our workforce today. You may start slowly at the beginning of the month but towards the end of the month (or worse, the quarter) you are working around the clock to make the numbers. Therefore, your standard day goes from eight hours to working twelve or more hours. I worked for a company that on Dec.31st the entire Finance department needed to be in the office to close the books and they celebrated the New Year by ordering pizza. Think of MURA being seasonal type work or extremes like the example of the Finance team.

2. **MURI** is the Japanese term meaning overburden: In today's corporate world, more than 80% of the people are multitasking or doing more than one person's job. Smart companies are figuring out that the employee's effectiveness at their job decreases the more they are burdened. Think of what multitasking really means…your brain is juggling different thoughts and focusing on nothing. A great example is going out with friends. How many times have you been talking to someone who is on his or her iPhone texting at the same time? How much do you really think they caught of your conversation? Next time this happens, ask them to repeat what you said…chances are they will not be able to or only repeat certain words. Which means you are going to have to tell them again and in Lean, this is considered a waste of your time!

3. **MUDA** is the Japanese term meaning waste: Identifying MURA and MURI are simpler than identifying MUDA. Lean gurus talk about "the eye on waste" observation style. In order to observe waste, you need to know what waste is. In a process, whatever the customer is not going to pay for is considered NVA, which, in turn is considered MUDA or waste. You can remember the types by using the acronyms TIM WOODS:

- **T**ransportation
- **I**nventory
- **M**otion
- **W**aiting
- **O**ver-production
- **O**ver-processing
- **D**efects
- **S**kills

Or DOWNTIME:

- **D**efects
- **O**ver-processing
- **W**aiting
- **N**ot using employees' talent (**S**kills)
- **T**ransportation
- **I**nventory
- **M**otion
- **E**xcessive production

In this book, we are going to go through the types of waste using "TIM WOODS".

Did you know that 90% of all work in the office is a Waste? Did you ever think that there are things you are doing which you believe are VA but really aren't? Remember, in Lean, the only VA is what the customer will pay you for. Unfortunately, the reality is there will always be tasks you will perform for business reasons, regardless if the customer does not pay for. A good example is marketing materials to get your business going. This brings value to you to get customers, but these customers aren't paying for the materials, just the product or service you provide. In this case, it is a necessary task or necessary NVA task, which cannot be eliminated but can be improved to reduce its costs. Another good example is internal meetings with no agendas and no takeaways. I remember one of my colleagues telling me after we had a meeting together "what was that about?" "Am I supposed to do something with this?" "I feel I just wasted time I'm not getting back." For an internal meeting to be VA it needs to relate directly to the customer with actions concerning the customer.

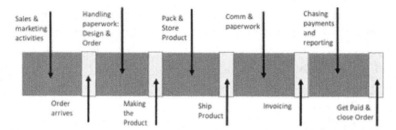

Let us look at an end-to-end value stream process. You can see more dark grey tasks than light grey in the diagram above for the process steps. This is because the customer is not paying for these steps, regardless if they are necessary for the company.

Any type of paperwork besides the order and the invoice are considered NVA.

16.1 Transportation

Is considered a waste because it can be an unnecessary cost absorbed by companies. Examples are:

- Employee travelling between offices: I spent over 2 hours each way going to my Boston office. So even though I would leave my home at 5am to get in by 7:30 due to traffic, I used to leave the office by 1 pm to avoid traffic going home and this meant that I could not do work until I got home. Lesson learned is that I was more productive in my home office.
- Documents' handling: sending drawings to our suppliers, customers or sister companies. UPS or FedEx are all expenses that could be avoided if we emailed or used a shared documentation software.
- Factory floor transporting of goods: transportation is all about moving the products from one station to another using equipment, like forklifts.

16.2 Inventory

If you change your paradigm and think of inventory as clutter, then you can truly see the waste in space and time spent locating something. Later on, in this book, you will learn of 5S+Safety, which is a Lean method of removing clutter. Some examples:

- Factory using the batch processing: Since Lean thinks of single piece flow, using first in first out, in order to avoid bottleneck as well as inventory, batching would be the opposite. Batching will open the door to higher inventory of product because you have a group of parts versus just one going through the process at a given time. Therefore, instead of having a pull system flow where the customer's request is filled, you are fulfilling the customer's request and the extra parts go to other customers or inventory. Moreover, if the stations the part needs to travel on the factory floor are performed at different speeds, there is more of a possibility a slower station will cause a bottleneck for all the parts, not just the one going to the customer.

- Your computer: How many of you have your email inbox with over 10 unread? Alternatively, you have all the emails you ever got still in your inbox. Your reasoning is so you can search. However, isn't the searching going to be longer than if you created folders for your information? You will waste time searching! Worse, you are using a lot of GB memory keeping all the emails, even the ones you will never go to again.

- Office inventory: imagine your work's supply closet is always messy. Going to get a pad or a pen will take you longer than if everything was in its own place. I've seen supply closets with old materials collecting dust and taking up space.

- Your garage: I'm sure I'm not the only one that had a messy garage, kept going to the hardware store to buy a hammer every time I needed it because I couldn't find it and when I finally organized my garage, found four hammers.

16.3 Motion

So many ask me what is the difference between transportation and motion? The easiest way for me to answer this is by example:

- Factory floor: some items need to move from the materials' store. You got to the store, collect the items you need, then place them in a container that you will transport to your station. All the movement you are doing is considered motion. If you were to use a forklift to move the items, then the transportation piece (i.e. forklift) would be the additional wasted cost.

- FedEx Documents: you know that using FedEx instead of electronic delivery is going to be transportation. But the fact you need to run down to the post office to get the documents to the FedEx counter is motion.

- Virtual Motion: think of how many things you need to click your mouse or go into various systems to accomplish a task. The more complex it is for a task to be completed, the more chances you have motion waste in your process. I worked for a company that had 386 different systems for just project management and a PM needed to know where to go in order to manage their project. Ridiculous!

16.4 Waiting

Do I really need to say more? The biggest waste in the office is waiting:

- Waiting for someone to answer your email. Why is this a waste and not part of life? Well, because if you are waiting on an answer from an email, you start doing something else. When you see that the answer has come in, you need to recalibrate your brain to what you needed to do for that item and go do it. There is a lot of back and forth. At the end of the day, if you cannot move on from completing something because you need to wait for someone, the waiting is considered a waste.
- Waiting on someone to start a meeting.
- Waiting in line to photocopy or pick up what you printed.
- Waiting for management to give you all the required signatures for approvals in order to start your project

Unfortunately, we have it hard cored in our makeup that waiting is equivalent to patience. We think of waiting as a normal occurrence or it is just part of life. In Lean, waiting for something is a disruption in the flow, therefore it is considered waste.

16.5 Over-production

This is the waste of producing more than you require. Examples are:

- How many of you found yourselves creating PowerPoint slides just for a meeting and they do not get used?
- Marketing prints out a thousand brochures because it cost them $0.02 less per print and then they are sitting on a shelf, collecting dust because only two hundred were required.
- Updating reports that you then send to everyone in the company but only a few key people really need to analyze them
- Each department has their own version of the same document. How do you think the customer feels going through your company's process and seeing that he needs

to adapt to every new form, each time he deals with a different department? Consistency, standardization and simplification are key requirements in Lean.

- Finally, who has received an email that was sent to everyone by mistake? Then you have various people "reply all" telling the sender they made the mistake. Not only do you get inventory in your email inbox of all the other emails, but you waste the time going through them before deleting them. No value to your work, just a disruption to it.

16.6 Over-Processing

What is the difference between over-processing and over-production? Well, in over-production we saw it is all about producing things not necessary. Over-processing is doing more than you need to in a process to make it work. Examples are:

- Factory: you are using a lathe to trim a piece of steel and then you file it down manually. Any type of rework is considered over-processing.
- Office: you received an email with a file attached. You copy it to your hard drive, then uploading it on a shared site and keeping the email. How many places do you need the same information? What can be worse is if you update the file and save it on one location. Then you go crazy trying to find the latest file.
- What about waiting around for approvals like those that we saw in "waiting waste". Do you need all those levels of approvals? Lean gives accountability and empowerment at all levels of the organization. You may need to go to your manager for some approvals, but you have a pre-defined approval matrix which gives some flexibility for you to go ahead if certain criteria are met.
- Restructuring a business: Yes, you read it correctly. Lean thinks of restructuring as waste. Why you may ask? Because people unsure of their livelihood in a company will be less productive, occupying their thoughts on whether or not they have a job, that they do not do their job fully focused.

16.7 Defects

Companies look at good /bad or right / wrong, but they don't always drill down into the defect to see if there are any defective(s). Why is it bad or wrong?

- Let us take for example order entry who enter orders for the salespeople. The process is that the salesperson gives the order entry person the customer's purchase order along with the quote. If the two documents do not match, then it is a defect. If we look closer and see that the "ship to" address, part numbers, pricing and terms &

conditions do not match. These four items are defectives. Fixing the defectives will fix the defect. Alternatively, the defect cannot be fixed unless the defectives are fixed first. In this example, the salesperson needs to understand what is required in these fields, thus fixing the defective in order to fix the defect.

- A defect can be something incomplete, something that is inaccurate or something that is not precise and needs clarification. In all three cases, you need to go back to the source to get it corrected. If you simply go back and tell them to correct it without informing them how to do it going forward, then you find yourself in a "Groundhog Day" syndrome where the same defect keeps happening.

Remember, if you catch the defect up front, then the costs are low. The simple 1-10-100 rule states **One dollar** spent on prevention will save **10 dollars** on correction and **100 dollars** on failure costs. Take the earlier example with order entry. If it gets caught at this point, then you can fix it with little cost. But if it slips to manufacturing, then the wrong part can be manufactured. To fix it at this point costs more money. Nevertheless, you still have control internally to fix it though it will cost you more in materials and time. However, if the wrong part ends up at the customer, then you are paying for all the work done to date, the return of the part, and redoing the whole order from scratch. In many cases, you need to deal with an unhappy customer that may not come back to you in the future. Defects need to be handled as soon as they are found!

16.8 Skills

The last type of waste is Skills or how "DOWNTIME" identifies this waste, "not using employee's talents". Examples are:

- Hiring a person to do one job, but then telling them to do something else.
- Inheriting someone else's responsibilities because they left the position and you are not trained to do the job
- Reporting to two different managers with conflicting views on what you need to accomplish
- Lack of direction in your role: do you know how you tie to the company's vision? In the past, I have heard of more "I don't know, I just work here" then reciting the vision.

If an employee is unhappy in their workplace and act out, before you remove them, drill down to the root of what makes them unhappy. Chances are they are doing something they did not believe they were going to do when they were hired. On the other hand, they can be bored in their current role and need a challenge. The waste here is more to the company than the employee is because the company is losing out fostering and developing their employee's skills.

Chapter 17: Gemba

A key principle from the Toyota Production System was Genchi Genbutsu Gemba:

- *Genchi Genbutsu* is a Japanese term meaning "Go and See."
- *Gemba* is another Japanese term meaning "real place" (where the work takes place).

The Toyota Production System (TPS) holds the key principle to use before you start drawing your process mapping. The inventor of TPS, Taiichi Ohno, was well known to take his apprentices to the shop floor, have them stand there and observe. In fact, he would actually use chalk to draw a circle on the floor and have them stand in the circle until his return. Once he returned, he would ask the apprentice what wastes he or she observed. If he was not satisfied with the answer, he left the apprentice there to observe some more. He was not being mean; he was applying a new form of discipline where instead of assuming how things worked, one needed to watch the process to understand what was actually happening. He wanted to make sure they lessoned to go to the source to understand them first.

Why is Genchi Genbutsu Gemba or simply Gemba important for you when mapping out your process? In chapter 4, we looked at the different types of processing mapping. You used the high-level process map in your SIPOC to visualize the main steps of the process. This visual is not enough to find waste.

Next time you have a chance, conduct an experiment where you observe people in a conference room discussing how things work and mapping out their perceived process. It will look similar to your SIPOC or this illustration below:

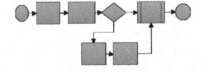

Go to the place where this process is actually being applied and write out the steps. Chances are you will end up with something more complex than the mapping in the conference room:

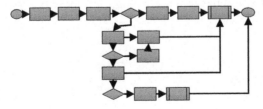

This is exactly what happens to me when I consult. The company gives me process maps telling me how it works. I go on site to see how this process is followed only to record a different process map than the one given to me. At the end of the day, you are targeting to have a flow process so it should look as linear as possible.

The goal for your journey is to start with a complex process map that you will streamline using Lean concepts and end up with a future state which flows and is simplified.

In order to prepare you, watch the following YouTube video link: https://www.youtube.com/watch?v=cq60dx1xjJw to witness a Dojo Gemba simulation at Toyota in Japan. This 4.15-minute-long video will show you how the trainees in this session are observing a man putting together a radiator. Notice that they are recording the steps and the time for each of the steps.

For your Gemba, you will be observing your process identified in the charter, QFD and / or the performance standards. You will require a stopwatch along with some paper and pen or pencil to record your observations. Go to Appendix B for a sample template you can use when going to the Gemba.

Here are some key points when you conduct your Gemba:

- Remember you are observing, not auditing or supervising, so DO NOT ask too many questions! During your observations you may have witnessed something unclear, you can ask them to clarify the step for you after the process steps are completed.
- Focus only on your project's key process.
- Tell the person you are observing that you are going to watch them run the process looking at time for each step and any potential wastes you can identify. Make sure they agree to be observed.
- Your Gemba should not take longer than a day, depends on your process.
- Don't forget to thank the person who allowed you to watch them work the process. If they are interested it what you are doing, definitely be open to share your results!

Chapter 18: Spaghetti Diagram

The spaghetti diagrams, also described as spaghetti charts, spaghetti plots, spaghetti drawing, or spaghetti models are used to look at the distance travelled when producing a product or service for the customer. It is visual way of showing what happens in the process when there are moving parts. It often answers the questions:

- Why are there so many moving parts?
- Why does it need to go back and forth?
- Why do we have so much travelling or motion waste?

The spaghetti diagram is not limited to manufacturing only. The applications are:

- Factory: draw layout of the equipment and how a part goes from one to the next
- Office: draw layout of desks, office equipment or departments. An example would be looking at how much motion exists when having one printer in the office.
- Software: draw the different software's you use to complete a process recording all the back and forth as well as clicks.
- Service: draw a layout of the locations a serviceman goes to when preparing to service a customer

Preparing and creating a Spaghetti Diagram for your process:

1. Procure something to draw on (paper, computer, etc.) and a pen or pencil
2. Have your Gemba results handy
3. Decide what your fixed locations will be and draw them as boxes on paper
4. Based on your observations, draw lines from one box to the next following the part, mouse, or person through the process. It is useful to number each line, so you retain the sequential flow
5. Question each line "will the customer pay for this?" is so, it is VA, if not it is NVA
6. Analyze the visual and see what wastes are occurring. Motion is definitely one of the wastes as soon as you see the going back and forth or long distances because you are wasting time
7. Calculate what percentage of NVA is occurring in the diagram

Here is a great 1.40-minute video on spaghetti diagrams:
https://www.youtube.com/watch?v=5QEHS5tieiU

In the "Improve Customer Responsiveness" project, we are going to put together a spaghetti diagram displaying the different systems the customer service representative needs to navigate when responding to a customer request. The customer is paying for the service of having his or her questions answered on the product they purchased. However, they are paying the representative to go to one place to get the answer for them, not multiple places and spending a lot of time to retrieve the information. So, along with the representative, a possible utopia process would be "Read the customer's request / answer the phone and listen to the customer, go into the company's system to find the order with the information and relay it to the customer" If you look at the current process, the representative is far from this utopia solution. Since the company's system is not trusted, the representative does more legwork to ensure the response is correct, and then goes back to the customer.

You can see from the illustration that there are four wastes identified from TIM WOODS wastes and the NVA in this diagram is at 82%. Since this example is clicking a mouse, there is no Transportation waste. In order to get to where the representative wants to be in the process, there is plenty of waste that needs to be removed.

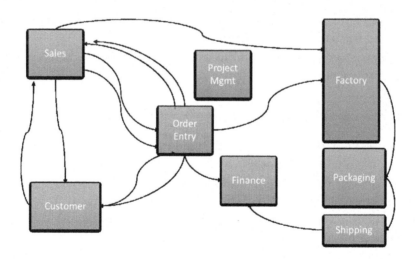

Chapter 19: VSM Current State

When you think of a value-stream map (VSM), you should think of a stream, which flows in one direction. If thinking of nature is difficult for you, think of the IKEA store with the arrows on the ground guiding you through the store or of a Disney amusement park where there are wooden arrows directing you on a sequence of rides. All these examples are showing you a one directional flow. In fact, if you have been to Disney, they do not only give you the flow of rides but even within each ride. They are able to give you a waiting time based on where you are standing in line.

There are two possible processes to follow when going from the current state VSM to the future state VSM. It's up to you which you prefer to use.

First possible VSM Process:

1. Product Families: the group of products or types of services that are going through the process you are wanting to improve. In many cases, you may have multiple products grouped into families following a process. In a factory, you have many products being built, but you are only going to concentrate on the product(s) going through the one process you want to improve. In the Office, you are looking into several departments' processes where more than one type of document goes through. Narrow down your product family to the documents going through one process which ties to your customer CTQs.
2. Current State Map: Once you decided on the product you will watch the flow of the process by going to the Gemba. The observations from the Gemba to map out the As-Is process.
3. Implementation Plan (PDCA): establish a PDCA place with measurable actions, owners and timeline. When the action is conducted, if it is a success and will strengthen your future state, then qualify and quantify it with the benefits it will yield. This is shown to you in Chapters 31, 32 and 33.
4. Future State Map: based on the PDCA results, come up with what your ideal to-be process by following the guide in Chapter 30.

Second possible VSM Process:

1. Product Families: the group of products or types of services that are going through the process you are wanting to improve. In many cases, you may have multiple products grouped into families following a process. In a factory, you have many products being built, but you are only going to concentrate on the product(s) going

through the one process you want to improve. In the Office, you are looking into several departments' processes where more than one type of document goes through. Narrow down your product family to the documents going through one process which ties to your customer CTQs.

2. Current State Map: Once you decided on the product you will watch the flow of the process by going to the Gemba. The observations from the Gemba to map out the As-Is process.

3. Future State Map: come up with what your ideal to-be process by following the guide in Chapter 30.

4. Implementation Plan (PDCA): establish a PDCA place with measurable actions, owners and timeline. When the action is conducted, if it is a success and will strengthen your future state, then qualify and quantify it with the benefits it will yield. This is shown to you in Chapters 31, 32 and 33.

Remember, create a VSM only once your GEMBA walk is completed. When drawing your VSM, LSS starts and ends with the customer. So, your customer should be drawn at the top and center of the process using the crown icon. Next you draw the flow of steps you observed. In addition, place the time each of the steps took. One of the reasons you record time is to have a numerical NVA calculation. When you go through each of the steps and identify which are VA/NVA, then using the time will help you calculate the NVA percentage. Placing time is a key difference between a VSM and the other process maps. It numerically tells you how good or bad your process is with respect to the customer and it visually displays how much NVA you have in the process, especially if you choose to color code every NVA in Red, Essential-NVA in Orange, and VA in Green. For a simple straight forward example, go back to Chapter 4 to see a VSM diagram.

The time you collected for the steps will also serve for looking at your process quantifiably:

- calculate how long your entire process is or its cycle time (C/T).
- calculate the processing time (P/T) which is only the time spent in the steps and excludes any waiting, motion or transportation time.
- calculate the Lead Time (L/T) which is the total time from the start of process with the customer to the delivery of product or service to the customer.
- calculate your process' takt time, which is shown in section 19.1

Keep in mind you are working on your first LSS project so the VSM you will be creating will be simple. There are courses, which focus on VSM building alone along with an array of icons. For your first time building a VSM, I will suggest using the most common icons found in Appendix B, which are coming from the Lean lexicon website.

When transferring your Gemba notes into a VSM, use a process tool. You can go online and download draw.io for free using its basic functionality or use software's like Visio or ARIS. Of course, you can always map the VSM in Excel or PowerPoint, but they will be more challenging to use since the not all the icons are included.

19.1 Takt Time

We first spoke of takt time back in Chapter 11. The takt time is calculated once you have drawn out your VSM.. This is basically looking at the time the work is done dividing it by the customer demand. For example, if I am building motors, and XYZ is my customer. XYZ requires 20 motors a week. We have 2 shifts of 8 hours each which means that our factory works on motors 80 hrs./week. Since XYZ wants 20 motors per week, the calculation is (80 hours/week) ÷ (20 motors/week) equaling 4 hours/motor. The takt time equation is:

$$\text{Takt Time} = \frac{\text{Effective working Time per Period}}{\text{Customer Demand per Period}}$$

A great way of explaining takt time in a workshop is by using a YouTube clip from "I love Lucy" tv showing her working in the chocolate factory. The YouTube link is:
https://www.youtube.com/watch?v=NkQ58I53mjk&t=5s
You see if you do not keep pace with the takt time, then you will end up being late with the customer request.

19.2 NVA Percentage

Once you mapped out your VSM, you want to calculate the VA and NVA cycle time so that you can know from your process what is the percentage of your NVA. Remember that if the customer does not pay for it, then it will be NVA. And if we need to do it internally due to policy or necessity, then it is essential-NVA. For the NVA percent calculation, the essential-NVA is considered NVA.

We have the NVA percent calculation below. You simply add up all of the NVA time you deemed would not be paid by the customer and divide it by the lead time:

$$\%NVA = \frac{NVA + Essential\ NVA}{VA + NVA + Essential\ NVA}$$

Value Stream Mapping can be simple like this example or very complex. There are specific courses and books just talking about VSM. I actually took a one-week course to go through all possible functionalities. This book is only scratching the surface with the basics.

ANALYZE PHASE

Now that you have collected your data and measured your current state, you are able to analyze your process.

Let us take the doctor example: your blood tests are in and your doctor is going to evaluate your situation to see how bad it is.

Chapter 20: Project Capability

When you are calculating capability, you are looking for the sigma value, DPMO and capability indices to help you understand how good your current process is today. Prior to statistical software's, like Minitab®, you needed to calculate the sigma value manually. We are not going to dive into the manual calculations in this book but keep it simple by using Minitab®. For the step-by-step instructions on how to get the capability report, go to Appendix A.

In order to understand the current process, you need to study the data by looking at the bell curve's shape, stability, spread and centering. You have already been analyzing your bell curve in the previous chapters when looking at the precision and accuracy.
In this chapter, we are going to be looking at what reports can be run to help you interpret your bell curve as well as understand your As-Is capability of your process.

20.1. Bell Curve Analysis

Keep in mind there are multiple reports you can use in this situation. We are going to take the simple and Lean route when interpreting our curve.

Shape: When you completed your Test Retest Study, you ran either the Descriptive Statistics report. The graphical view quickly gave you an indication how proportional your bell curve was. It also showed the bar chart, which built your curve so that you can understand where most of your data lies. This helps you determine if your curve is skewed.

Spread: When you completed your Test Retest Study, you ran either the X-bar or I-bar chart to let you know whether your process was in control. You also used the Mean to calculate how accurate you were with your process. You recall that accuracy looks at on average how close are you to the target because most of your data is scattered. Thus, the more your data points are scattered around, the more chances you have a spread issue. The Descriptive Statistics report will confirm it visually as well as the Capability report we are going to look at in the next section.

Centering: If your precision test failed; chances are your bell curve is off-center. Remember the centering really depends on your target. The Capability report will also give you a better visual of the performance standards you have decided in the previous chapter. Since you may have completed your Test Retest Study without the final target and specification limits.

Stability: We use control charts to determine the stability of a process. If you are out of control, then there is no stability. This means that if you went and collected new data points, they would give you different results from the previous ones. Besides the X-bar or I-bar, we are going to look at the Capability report, which will include either the P-chart or the X-bar - R charts.

Since you are looking at your current state process, your bell curve will not be perfect. It will have one or more of the four types just described above showing you where the variation lies. The idea is to know what problems your bell curve has and target those areas for improvement so that in turn you decrease the variation.

20.2 Capability Indices

There are four performance capability indicators which help you understand your process' performance and variation. The capability indices (Cp and Cpk) and the performance indices (Pp and Ppk) are the most common.
Take as an illustrated example your descriptive statistics bell curve where the tails of the curve on either side are your upper and lower specification limits. The aim of course, is to remain within the specifications from your performance standards which tie with your customer's CTQs specifications.

The calculations for these indices are using the Mean, standard deviation and specification limits. Now to better understand the formulas that calculate these indices, go to isixsigma.com website. Here we are going to describe the two main indices you will be interpreting in your capability report: Cpk and Ppk. Both indices produce a numerical ratio telling you how close your target is to your Mean using the specification limits. The main differences are:

Cpk index is the process capability index:

- looks at variation within the subgroups, but not between the subgroups of your data population extracted from your process
- some target Cpk of 1.33 or greater so that you know your process meets the customer's CTQs. In some industries, the ration is higher at 1.66
- tells you where your potential capability lies over time.

Ppk index is the process performance index:

- looks at the overall variation – both within and between the subgroups of your data population extracted from your process
- will tell you how much of a shift there is between the subgroups

- tells you where you are with your process.

Many only look at the Cpk, but you cannot discard the Ppk unless the both the Cpk and the Ppk have similar ratios. When the two are similar or identical, it tells you that the average standard deviation is the overall standard deviation. These are known when you run the capability analysis.

20.3 Capability Analysis for Continuous Data

Minitab® version 17 and older will reveal a flowchart that asks you which of the data types you have for your project. If you have continuous data, then you are able to run the Capability Analysis report. Go to Appendix A for the step-by-step instructions. When you run this report, you will get the following reports:

- Process Performance Report
- Summary Report
- Diagnostic Report
- Report Card

Let us go through each of your output reports and interpret what you are seeing.

20.3.1 Process Performance Report

The graphical view will show two views of your process' bell curve in the histogram:
- the solid line is your actual capability, also known as the overall experience your customer is feeling
- the dotted line is your potential capability or within what can be achieved if you removed the noise variation.

On the right-hand side you will see the statistics which include:
- Mean
- Standard deviation overall and within subgroups
- Actual (overall) process:
    - o Pp and Ppk
    - o Z bench also known as your sigma value
    - o Percentage you are out of specification as observed and expected
    - o DPMO as observed and expected
- Potential (within) process:
    - o Cp and Cpk

- o   Z bench also known as your sigma value
- o   Percentage out of specification expected
- o   DPMO expected

We reviewed the differences between the performance indexes at the beginning of this chapter. Ideally you can only focus on the Cpk if both the Ppk and Cpk ratios are close. Remember, if they are different, you need to look at each and not discard what the Ppk is telling you. Put in simple terms, the Ppk using the within and overall standard deviations to do the calculation while Cpk only uses the within and estimates as an average the overall. If the shift and drift is small, Ppk and Cpk are almost equal, then Cpk is a good valid number, because there is no big distinction between the within and overall standard deviations. The Z bench numbers are considered the sigma values. Now depending what you read in statistics, you will see that some use the 1.5 shift for the short-term sigma value, and some don't. Since we are using Motorola's model for stats, we will add the 1.5 shift to the short-term.

The short-term sigma value is the Z bench overall or actual found with the Ppk calculation. This is found to be more reliable than the long-term because of many possible changes which can occur over time to a process. To equalize these changes, we add the 1.5 shift. The long-term sigma value is the Z bench within, or potential found with the Cpk calculation. This is more of what can be expected if no changes occur in the process as time passes.

20.3.2 Summary Report

The summary report is where you will retrieve your DPMO along with your Z bench or sigma value along with your DPMO so you can statistically describe your current state process. Now it really is up to you if you want to add the 1.5 shift or not when quantifying your As-Is. Regardless, this is your starting point. Towards the end of this book, you will be rerunning this report to see if the numbers improved, thus reducing the variation to your process.

The graphical bell curve here is more pronounced showing you exactly how you're your process is with respect the upper and lower specification limits from your customer CTQs. The percent defective is the average percentage of items in your sample size that are considered unacceptable or fall outside the specification limits. As a rule of thumb, the smaller the percentage, the better it is because you are satisfying your customers. When you compare the percentage defectives with the target percentage, i.e. 2.5% for lower limit and 2.5% for upper limit yielding the 5% alpha (described in more detail in Chapter 25) having your percent defective greater than the alpha indicates you need to improve your process.

20.3.3 Diagnostic Report

Here is where you find the control charts and the probability curve. The control charts will tell you if your process is stable and in control. Minitab® is already using the control chart guidelines in its calculations so if you have any red dots on your graph you will automatically know you are not stable, and thus, out of control.

The Normality test reveals the probability curve along with the P-value. The rule is that your data is normally distributed if the P-value is greater than 0.05. Minitab® later version will also spell it for you stating "pass" or "fail" results.

20.3.4 Report Card

Finally, you get from Minitab® a summary of all that was seen previously in a report card. It looks at:

- Stability: being stable will eliminate any special cause variation in your process
- Number of subgroups: this looks at your data source and compares to the recommended 25 subgroups or more to capture reliable process variation
- Normality: passing this test will yield an accurate capability result
- Amount of Data: ideally you always want continuous data which is greater than 100 data points. Here it compares to your data source to capture precision

20.4 Binomial Capability for Discrete Data

When you cannot get continuous data and are working with discrete data, then the best approach to use so you can retrieve your DPMO and sigma value is running the Binomial capability report. Go to Appendix A for the step-by-step instructions.

When you run this report, you will get the following reports:

- Summary Report
- Diagnostic Report
- Report Card

20.4.1 Summary Report

The summary report is where you will retrieve your DPMO along with your Z bench or sigma value along with your DPMO so you can statistically describe your current state process. This Z bench overall is considered short-term sigma value which is found to be more reliable than the long-term because of many possible changes which can occur over time to a process. To equalize these changes, we usually add the 1.5 shift. Now it really is up to you if you want to add the 1.5 shift or not when quantifying your As-Is. Regardless, this is your starting point. Towards the end of this book, you will be rerunning this report to see if the numbers improved, thus reducing the variation to your process. So just remember to compare apples to apples, either adding the shift both before and after, or not.

The graphical is a bar graph along with arrange line on the top showing you exactly where the % defectives are on average. It is a depiction of the percentage of defectives found in each sub-group. The line on the top is where most of the defectives reside and the remaining are found outside the average. Keep in mind that Minitab® will tell you that if you exceed the % defectives acceptable, you are required to improve your process because it is not fulfilling the customer's requirements.

Finally, on the top right-hand side there is a barometer visual that tells you if the percent defective is within or less than 50% in your process. Greater than the 50% means your process is not acceptable as-is because it does not meet the customer requirements. You need to look into what your defectives are and fix them to keep your process from having all that noise variation.

20.3.3 Diagnostic Report

This report shows you the P-chart and cumulative percent defective of your process. Just like all the other control charts, Minitab® is using the control chart guidelines in its calculations so if you have any red dots on your graph you will automatically know your process is not stable, and thus, also out of control.

The P-chart looks at process stability. As long as you see no dots red or outside the range, then your process is stable.

The cumulative percent defective chart will give you the percentage of your defectives on average by depicting a horizontal line across the chart. Remember that as a rule of thumb you require to have less than 50% in order to have your process accepted.

20.3.3 Report Card

The report card is a summary of all the pieces in the report we have just gone through. It looks at:

- Stability: the proportion of defective data points are either stable and in control or unstable, thus out of control
- Number of subgroups: this looks at your data source and compares to the recommended 25 subgroups so to have a good representation of your process
- Expected variation: whenever your data's variation varies from the expected variation; the control charts are not going to be accurate
- Amount of Data: it looks at the 95% confidence interval for the percent in defectives. When this is too wide, it asks to collect more data for this test to increase the precision.

Chapter 21: Fishbone Diagram – Looking at Causes

Kaoru Ishikawa developed the Fishbone Diagram in the 1960's as part of a trailblazing quality control program for manufacturing environment. It may also be called the Cause & Effect diagram or Ishikawa Diagram. I find this to be the cheapest root cause methods out there that really does work. Though it was a not part of the TPS (Toyota Production System), it was quickly adopted by Lean practitioners. Thus, it's being used today in both the Six Sigma and Lean environments so it's safe to say it should be in your Lean Six Sigma toolkit.

It's a structural approach to solving a complex project, used in a team setting in order to get everyone to brainstorm together. It expands your thinking with the hope that you think out of the box. Visual view listing all of your project's possible causes to your problem. Once you have your FMEA, the NVA identified through the VSM and Wastes seen when going to the Gemba, you now have a good chunk of causes or issues for your project. Let us go through the steps for building your fishbone.

Step 1: Draw the blank skeleton diagram

We start by using a skeleton which looks similar to the diagram below and has six possible cause types: Measurements, Methods, Materials, Machines, People, and Environment. The effect is going to be your problem statement.

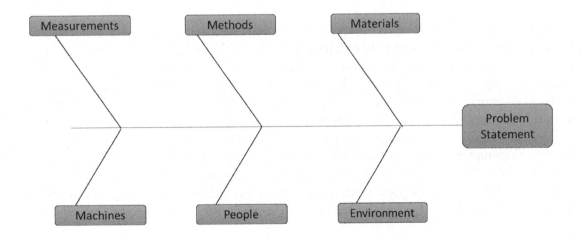

When building a fishbone, I always tell people to look at this as a template which can be changed. If you don't have six types or groupings for your causes, but four, then list only four. Same occurs if you have seven instead of six. Definitely tailor this fishbone to your project and do not limit yourself thinking that these are the only possible cause types.

Remember this is a starting point so to get you thinking. Some have placed employees, suppliers, policies, procedures, plant, equipment, etc. instead of the six types you see here. Therefore, if the cause types above do not pertain to your project, type the ones that do. Ask the team, what are the main causal groupings? Sometimes you may start it thinking it's a possible cause, then you find that nothing gets grouped under this cause. Maybe you have reasons for the problem happening that do not fall in any other the groups, you can also create a "Other" causal group so you can place the one offs.

Step 2: Label the Problem statement

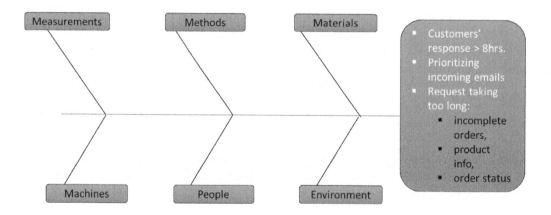

Next you label your fishbone's problem statement. Let's take the Improve Customer Responsiveness project. The baseline charter had the problem statement "Unevenness in responding to customers depending on the type of request. Currently we respond to ~385 request per day by email and phone calls." but after iterations based on the learnings, the problem statement now looks like: "Customers' complain that their emails are not being responded to on the same day. Internally there are issues with customer service representatives' prioritizing incoming emails. Furthermore, the top three types of customer requests (incomplete orders, product info, order status) make up 75% of the overall cycle time shift." You can see that this is a long problem statement. So, you can see here I shortened it by placing it as point form format. Remember, this problem needs to be clear to the team so that they can brainstorm the correct causes that they believe have created this problem statement.

Step 3: Label the Cause Types

Sometimes, it's easier to label the cause types on the fishbone once you and your team have brainstormed all possible causes simply because you can group the causes brainstormed and use what you decide to title the group as the cause type.

In anticipation for your brainstorming meeting, consolidate for the team the latest FMEA, the wastes I identified when going to the Gemba and the NVA we found when we did the VSM. This way, you have a starting point for possible causes on your fishbone. Sometimes it is good to prepare questions to instigate your team to think of all causes. In this example, the questions would be:

- "Why do we close out our requests so late?"
- "Why do incomplete orders take so long?"
- "Why do product information take so long
- Why does finding the order status take so long?"
- "How are we prioritizing the emails today?"
- "Are our systems slowing us down?"
- "Do you think we need training?"
- "Why is this happening?"

Based on the brainstorming that was done in this example, the labels have slightly changed. See here how the "Machines" type is changed to "Systems". This occurred because we deal with outlook for emails, ERP for logging and skype for chatting with people internally. The project is not a factory or warehouse project looking at machines. So, using the word "Systems" is relatable to everyone on the team. Similarly, "Measurements" changed to "Response time" because that is the only measurement we are concerned with and we don't want to get sidetracked thinking of other things we can measure. Finally, we deleted "Materials" because it's not needed and replaced it with the miscellaneous bucket of "Other" just in case someone comes up with some because that doesn't go in any of the other buckets.

Step 4: Label the branches

Place the causes that were grouped for the cause type, one per branch on the fishbone.

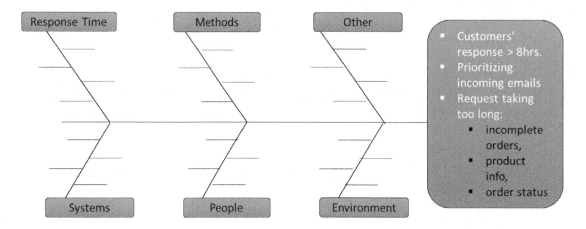

Step 5: Team Results

Here is the example of a fishbone filled out with some of the information. In no way is this a complete view and you should be doing the same amount of causes for each of the causal groupings.

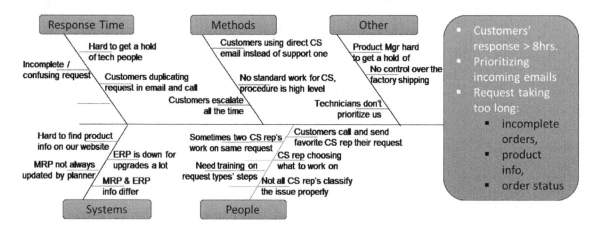

Since we are in the Analyze phase, keep in mind we have not finished going through the fishbone tool. Think of this as part one and part two will be completed in the Improve phase when we start looking at solutions.

Chapter 22: Root Cause Analysis

Let us recap what we have accomplished so far. In the Measure Phase, you mapped your current process along with the wastes; you translated the VoC into project deliverables; you established your performance standards and you validated your Measurement System Analysis.

In the Analyze Phase, you will identify why the wastes exist, why the defect is occurring and determine the root cause. We will be using both Six Sigma for statistical analysis and Lean for root causing the defect. This phase will help you prepare for the Improve phase by deep diving into possible defectives that have your defect occurs. In Essence, what you discover in Analyze will be what you will be problem solving and piloting in the Improve phase.

There are numerous Root-Cause Analysis (RCA) methodologies out there. All these methods help you brainstorm opportunities of solving your problem. Some of these methods require you to be certified in. In this book, we will be looking into certain methods you can quickly adopt at your workplace. Some we have already gone through:

- CTQ Drill Down Tree
- FMEA
- Eight steps of problem-solving
- 5 Why's
- So, What
- What if
- Fishbone

When looking into the root-cause of your problem statement, there are five logical steps you go through by answering specific questions:

- Step 1: What is the Problem? What do you see happening today? What are the symptoms?
- Step 2: What proof do you have that the problem exists? What is the impact of this problem? Do you have data collected?
- Step 3: What sequence of events lead to the problem? Identifying the possible causal factors. What other problems surround this issue? What are the conditions?
- Step 4: What is the reason the problem occurred? Why does the causal factor exist?

- Step 5: What do you recommend so that the problem does not reoccur? What can we do? Who will be responsible for implementing? How do we implement?

If you are able to answer these questions for your project, then you are able to successfully complete an RCA.

22.1 5 Why's

Usually this works when you have one failure mode you wish to drill down to its root cause. The good news is that anyone can use this method. In fact, we start doing using this method when we are toddlers. Unfortunately, as we become adults, we lose the curiosity and inquisitive thinking and get into a "status quo" mentality of "this is how it works here". A simple example has the problem being "the printer does not work":

Why is the Printer not working? **Because** there is no power going to the Printer…
Why is no power going to the Printer? **Because** the electrical cord got pulled out… Now here is where many people stop. But is this the true root cause? Let's continue…
Why did the electrical cord get pulled out? **Because** someone tripped on it… Wait a minute
Why did someone trip on it? **Because** the cord is too long…
Why is the cord too long? **OMG** the electrical outlet is across from the Printer!

Instead of doing the solution of just plugging the receptacle in the socket, you are actually going to be fixing the issue by either moving the printer or placing a new outlet next to it. If you stopped before getting to the root cause, this issue would happen again. There are definitely things that you see happening over and over again. Some of these things may actually be your pet peeves. Well, think of using this tool otherwise you may not be solving your issue.

Remember to go until you have asked 5 why's. If you end up continuing to ask and feel you are going in circles, then your cause is too complex to be solved with this method. A simple way of figuring out if you have reached your root cause is by going backwards and placing "therefore" to your original "why's". It would go like this:

Root-Cause: The electrical outlet is across from the Printer

- Therefore, the cord is too long
- Therefore, someone tripped on it
- Therefore, the electrical cord got pulled out
- Therefore, no power going to the Printer
- Therefore, the Printer not working

You can see that the logic sticks, so your root cause is viable.

22.2 So What?

The appreciation tool also known as "so what?" is very similar to the 5 why. It was developed by the military to gain a better understanding of a fact, statement or problem. You basically ask, "So what?" until the response is important to the situation. It is understandable, that you may find this offensive or negative because it does sound like a teenager with attitude, but it does actually work. In fact, I had a "So What?" poster in my office because when my employees came in with a problem, I expected them to also have a possible solution.

Now let's go through an example. The issue is the Printer not working:

So What? **So,** I can't print out my expense report
So What? **So,** that my manager approves my expense
So What? **So,** I get paid for my out of pocket money
So What? **So,** I can pay my debt
So What? **So,** I need to get the printer fixed

Cause: What's important is getting the money to pay the debt, so what needs to be done is fix the printer.

22.3 What If

The "What – If" is another great brainstorming technique. It looks at changing a piece of the proposed solution to see if it affects the overall. For example, if we add a new customer service representative, will that help with faster response time? When we play out the scenario, this person is going to either follow the same process or created their own. If the process they create, which is considered ad-hoc, does make them go faster, then they will respond to the customer's requests they handle faster. Following the same process will have them take the same time as the others to close a request. But keep in mind, even if they go faster, that is one person working ad-hoc within an entire group so chances are the overall variation will still exist. Thus, this is not a viable solution.

The idea here is to brainstorm all possible solutions to the issue and then theoretically explore the outcome if that solution were in place. Let us use the customer service representative example again but instead of adding an additional headcount, we decide to establish a script for the possible requests coming in so that they are consistent with responding to the customer and they follow a standard? What if a script was in place, would it reduce the cycle time responding to the customers? Play out the scenario and if this would reduce the cycle time then it should be on your Action log to test through PDCA.

Now let's go through an example. The issue the project team has a hard time getting together for weekly meetings:

What if we met first thing in the morning? Our group meeting is at that time; NOT Viable
What if we met at 4pm before people go home? People often come in earlier and leave earlier; NOT Viable
What if we met at lunchtime? Most can do this time since meetings are usually not scheduled; Viable

Decision: to pick a lunchtime that everyone usually has free during the week for the team meeting.

Chapter 23: Courageous Conversation™ (CC)

Courageous Conversation™ wording was trademarked when it was founded in 1992. It is used as a communication vehicle to resolve conflicts.

The three goals are to:

- Gain wisdom: broaden your perspective by listening
- Gain understanding: see the situation in the other person's perspective
- Gain knowledge: now that you gained the wisdom and understanding, you have the knowledge to resolve the issue

Start by understanding who you are planning to have this conversation with:

- What has occurred between you both?
- What will happen if you do not have this conversation?
- And what is important in keeping this relationship?

When you are using CC, it is important not to confront the other party only to play the blame game or judge their view as inferior. Remove all those strong negative emotions, i.e. screaming at the person. Think of the mantra of a yoga instructor, "Find your core". Stay respectful; speak facts so you both agree on what actually did occur and what is at stake if you do not come to an agreement. Remember, be positive!

The way we are going to approach, CC is by using a script, just to get you going, giving you, some talking points. Once you have done this a couple of times, you may find your way of coming across with your message.

- It begins with "When I observed…." and you recount the incident including how you interpreted the person's behavior.
- Next, you continue with "I feel…" sharing how this affects you. Remember to be specific about your state of mind.
- Then you go into what matters to you by starting with the phrase "Because I believe or value…" You want to make sure it is not only about them. You were there too so taking a piece of the responsibility.

- You complete the conversation by sharing a proposed solution emphasizing on the benefits on both sides. Make sure you remain open to new outcomes; just because you have, a solution does not mean the other party will accept it. You may end up have a conversation and coming up together with a new one.

Here is an example of the CC when I was facilitating a series of events. I saw someone in the team continually being disruptive. This was how I approached them after the workshop:

CC: I observed in San Marcos and now Somerset's workshops you are on your computer disengaged by the discussions. When asked to participate, you responded with negative statements, like 'it's not going to work' and 'you guys don't know what you're talking about.'

I felt that instead of moving ahead with the exercise, some started arguing with you. Your disruptive behavior has affected the entire team and project.

This program came to be because you passionately wanted to solve this long-standing issue; I want to understand what happened that changed your position from a promoter to a detractor on this program. As one of the facilitators, I would like to help. How can I support you so this program can succeed?

Maybe we can get together before our next workshop to go through the logistics.

Outcome: after listening to the person for a while, we agreed on making sure this person was aware when it was happening, so we decided on a code word. In addition, our facilitation team had someone work closely with her for the remaining sessions.

Remember to be effective, you need to:

- Be specific in your observations; avoid being generalized
- Use one to up to three observations, don't create laundry list of incidents
- Pause to allow the other to respond
- Accept other possible outcomes
- Achieve agreement and closure

Chapter 24: Conflict Resolution Diagram (CRD)

We will begin this chapter going through the Thomas-Kilmann model, which shows the five different ways you can tackle a conflict.

Note: the graph goes from uncooperative to cooperative types on the x-axis, and from unassertive to assertive way of confronting on the y-axis.

The five ways you may approach a conflict are:

- Avoiding: you act like nothing has occurred; when you avoid, you are just delaying...hoping it goes away
- Accommodating: you want to just give them what they want, so you yield
- Compromise: you try to find a middle ground where you give something up to come to a solution
- Compete: your goal is to win the argument; this is sometimes called forcing
- Collaborate: you are trying to find a win-win situation, where both parties work in partnership to get to a joint solution

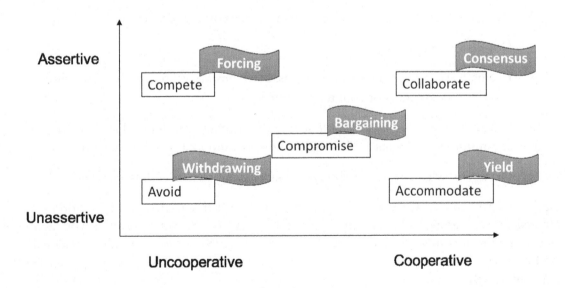

Think if conflict as an ingredient to your project instead of an obstacle. Whenever you are in a conflict, do not shy from it. You may retreat because you find you are not ready to engage. This is a good strategy, wanting to collect your emotions and come up with a game plan.

The CRD or Conflict Resolution Diagram, referred to as the Evaporating Cloud, is a tool that will help structure the conflict, focus on each position and look at the needs that drive both parties to a common objective. The steps you follow when putting together the CRD are shown here:

1. Articulate the Conflict: What is the position or demand of each person
2. Determine underlying need that drives the position
3. Evaluate the entire relationship
4. Develop assumptions
5. Evaluate assumptions
6. Create ideas (injections) on having the conflict evaporate
7. Decide on what type of method you will be using to deal with the conflict

Go to Appendix B to find a CRD sample template you can use for your project. It includes a sequential numbering displaying each step you need to take to complete the template. Fill out the CRD template as follows:

1. Articulate the Conflict: What is the position, demand or prerequisite of each person…

2. Determine underlying need that drives the position

3. Evaluate the entire relationship: do they have a comment objective?

4. Develop assumptions

5. Evaluate assumptions: look at which assumptions are valid (which means there are no counterarguments or counter examples.)

6. Create options (or injections) on having the conflict evaporate: challenge the assumptions, find what really is behind the assumptions, do the "what if's" scenarios.

7. Decide on what type of method you will be using to deal with the conflict

Both the CRD and the CC work when dealing with conflict. Another good method is Crucial Conversations by Kerry Patterson and I do suggest you get the book if you are in the midst of a lot of conflict or find the two methods presented not to your liking. Personally, I prefer using CC when I have a one-on-one situation and the CRD when more parties in my team are involved.

Chapter 25: Hypothesis Testing

Hypothesis testing is all about finding statistical significance by taking a small sample size from the overall data population. You want to see if what you want your process to do really can be done. It determines the probability of the hypothesis being true i.e. if you want to know that regardless when you extract the data, you will always have the same Mean or the same Variance. The best-case scenario is to have:

- The Mean close or on target
- Both Means of the operators the same
- Both Variances of the operators the same
- The Variance as small as possible with good confidence levels

Hypothesis testing establishes a confidence level in our data source, hence the likelihood of how our process is performing. For example, management tells you that you need to reach a certain target, say being 95% on-time with deliveries. When you perform the hypothesis test, you find that you cannot do that with the existing process. Management needs to be told that in order to get to 95% the process needs to be improved or redesigned.

Let us look at some sources of variation:

1. **Process Mapping**: we consider waste as a form of variation. Then mapping out your process will visually display the variation through **NVA** work being done.
2. **FMEA**: we consider failures as a form of variation. Identifying and pro-actively reducing or eliminating the **failures** will avoid any additional problems occurring on your project.
3. **Fishbone (Ishikawa)**: thoroughly breaks down the problem's **defects**, which creates variation.
4. **Pareto charting**: for prioritizes and narrows the focus on **defectives**, which in turn will affect the defect that creates variation.

Good news is you have already tackled these types of variations. Keep in mind, there are the overarching possible variations we covered in Chapter 14:

- Human error
- Equipment variability
- Environment variability
- Measurement variability

- Material variability
- Method variability

Keep all of these possible variations in your mind now that we enter hypothesis testing. Hypothesis testing looks at checking if your assumptions on the process are correct by using two data sets from your data source. Ideally, you want one of these two possible outcomes to occur:

- Null hypothesis (Ho) implies that the two sets of data yield the same results and we are assuming this is true, unless proven otherwise. Think of Ho being your ideal status quo for your project.

  - Formula: $\mu 1 = \mu 2$ or $\mu 1 - \mu 2 = 0$

- Alternative Hypothesis (Ha) implies that the two sets of data do not yield the same outcome. Therefore, you are rejecting your status quo (Ho) and accept the alternative hypothesis which may be that it's not possible to reach your desired target.

  - Formula: $\mu 1 \neq \mu 2$ or $\mu 1 - \mu 2 \neq 0$

You know we do not live in a black and white world, even though we may wish we did. There are grey areas when it comes to hypothesis testing. These grey areas are considered errors that may occur because of your data sets:

- Type one error or alpha (α) looks at the probability of accepting the alternative as your status quo even though the null hypothesis is true.
- Type two error or Beta (β) is the probability of accepting your null hypothesis which is your status quo while your alternative is true.

Keep in mind the main rules for these errors:

1. you cannot have both errors at once.
2. The alpha value is equal to the p values you will see in Minitab® and thus is considered to be 0.05 as a value.
3. The Power of the data is equal to one minus beta. This will show the relationship between the power and the sample size, when you are considering the Mean to a target.

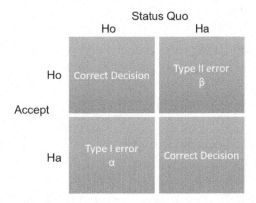

Here are the possibilities you have when conducting a hypothesis test. Remember we are looking at either accepting the hypothesis and believing it is status quo or not accepting the hypothesis and believing it is something different than the status quo.

But what if you don't get the answer you wanted in the results? So, you are tending towards not accepting the hypothesis given to you. Well, first you need to consider if your MSA passed the gage R&R. If the MSA gage did not pass, the hypothesis results are going to be at most directional, but definitely not reliable. Then you need to judge what to decide. And those are the two error type options: alpha and beta errors.

Let us use an example that was pasted on from one of my instructors in the past to help understand the possible choices in hypothesis testing. Think of a person being accused for a robbery. The four-box diagram would be:

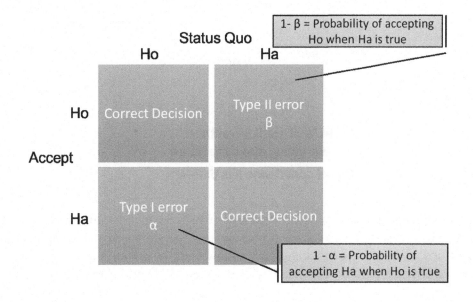

The black and white choices are the following:

- The person is innocent and so they are set free
- The person is guilty and so they are going to jail

With the introduction of possible errors, there are two more possibilities:

- The person is innocent and yet is going to jail
- The person is guilty and yet they are set free

The reason why you went through the Test Retest Study and the Gage R&R Study is to ensure your MSA is as reliable as possible so that these errors are as small as possible, if they even exist. If the studies were not conducted or your MSA did not pass, then the data sample size we are measuring is not reliable and chances are you are going to get an alpha or beta choice when you run the hypothesis testing.

Let us look at the errors in more depth to understand where they statistically come from. The alpha error can be described as the ends of the bell curve, outside the 95% confidence area. You can see from the diagram below that if you are within the 95% confidence area, your hypothesis Ho will manifest in your results. If you are outside this confidence area, then it'll be your Ha that will show up in your results.

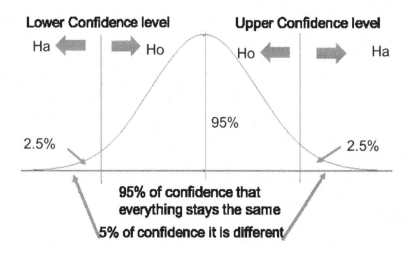

There is that remaining 5% or 2.5% on either side which creates that grey area where you may get the Ho as results but in reality, you are getting the alpha error. The alpha error is easily identified when you are looking at the p-value comparison in your results. This is why you are asked that any p-value less than 0.05 is considered Ha and not the Ho.

Looking at different data samples, this will show the relationship between Power, sample size and the difference when you are considering the means to a target. In simple terms, we are looking at the two errors which occur between the means. The alpha error is as we previously discussed, the needs of your bell curve, lying right outside the 95% confidence area. And so, we use the p-value when we run statistical reports to avoid getting this error. The beta error, on the other hand, comes about when you do not have enough data points to accurately run hypothesis tests. To understand the Power of your data, you need to run the 1-Sample t Test in Minitab®. This test works in two ways: will give you the number of data points that you need to run the hypothesis testing accurately and will give you the percentage of Power your actual data set has before running the hypothesis testing. The rule of thumb is to have a power value of 90% or greater to avoid the beta error from manifesting in your results.

The hypothesis testing process we are going to use in this book will be running the following Minitab® statistical reports:

1. **Descriptive Statistics**: to see whether your data is normally distributed or not
2. **1-Sample t Test**: to understand your level of Power in your data and be able to go get more data points, if needed, before entering hypothesis testing so that the beta error does not manifest itself.
3. **1-Variance Report**: to compare variances. When looking at your p-value, use:
    a. the Chi-Square results if your data is Normal
    b. the Bonett Method results if your data is Non-Normal
4. **Test for Equal Variances**: use the Levene Test p-value to determine your hypothesis outcome. Here you are looking at having the same amount of variance in the two data sets you use which come from your data source. You want to make sure that the variance is always the same, regardless when you pull your data from your process.
5. **Testing depends on the distribution:**
    a. **ANOVA Method for Normal data:** compare the Means of the two data sets to ensure they are equal throughout your process.
    b. **Mood Median for Non-normal data:** compare the Medians of the two data sets to ensure they are equal throughout your process.

Let us go into each of the above tests in more detail. Go to Appendix A for the step-by-step instructions. As it was stated throughout the Measure and Analyze phases, continuous data is the best. This would help because you can extract two or more samples of data within the total population. If you have discrete data, you will be limited in your samples, but the tests should still reveal results as long as your MSA passed.

25.1 Descriptive Statistics

Good news, you have already run the basic statistics in your Test Retest Study so as long as the data you are using is the same, you do not need to run this test again. Go to the summary view to see if your alpha or p-value > 0.05. If this is correct, your data is normally distributed and thus you can consider your null hypothesis to be correct. On the other hand, if your p-value was smaller than 0.05, then your data is not normally distributed and thus your alternative hypothesis should be accepted.

25.2 1-Sample t Test

Now that you know what your normality results are, you will test for your power value and for your required data points to keep from having the beta error manifesting.

    a. Getting your Power Value – When running this test in Minitab®, here are your inputs:
        i. Sample Size: type in your total amount of data points you plan to use for running the hypothesis tests
        ii. Difference: Take Mean (you get from Descriptive statistics results) and subtract it from your target Mean
        iii. Standard Deviation: take this from your Descriptive statistics results
        iv. Power Value: keep this field blank since this is what you want to know from the results. Remember that the percentage should be 90% or greater, anything lower than 90% will mean that there is a chance the Beta error will manifest in your hypothesis results.
    b. Getting your ideal number of data points required to run the hypothesis tests – When running this test in Minitab®, here are your inputs:
        i. Power Value: Use the 90% as your target power value
        ii. Difference: Take Mean (you get from Descriptive statistics results) and subtract it from your target Mean
        iii. Standard Deviation: take this from your Descriptive statistics results
        iv. Sample Size: keep this field blank since this is what you want to know from the results. If possible, comply with this number and make sure that when running the hypothesis tests, you have enough data so that you do not have the Beta error from manifesting.

25.3 1-Variance Report

When comparing variances, make sure you know whether your data is normal or not, so you select the correct results to interpret. Run the 1-Variance report in Minitab® to test the variability of consistency of performance from the various groups. Here the Ho you want to know is if your specified target will be possible with your process. If your p-value is greater than the 0.05, then your Ho is accepted and thus, the target is possible. If the p-value is less than the 0.05, then you are to accept the Ha or alternative hypothesis which is you are not going to be able to make your target with the process. Note that if you end up with a value less than 0.05, then you need to rethink your target. You may be too aggressive with what you have today as a process so it's not achievable at the moment. There is so much variation in your process and you may need to do baby steps to get there.

25.4 Test for Equal Variances

Next, we are testing to see if regardless of your data sets you pulled from your process, the variance is consistently the same throughout your process. This is your Ho. Your alternative Ha will be if the variance is different within your process. If this occurs, it means that your process is experiencing more variance sometimes and less in others. This also makes it harder to pinpoint the variance and decrease it because you may only be tackling some of it from your process. The test results will give you a p-value. The variances are considered the same as long as p-value is greater than 0.05. In addition to the p-value, the results depict a top view of a bell curve (so you see a line) for each of the sample sets. If these lines overlap, there is a good chance your variances are the same.

25.5.1 ANOVA Method for Normal data

If you have normal data, then you will be looking to see if the average of each of your data sets is the same. In other words, you are comparing the Means of the two data sets to ensure they are equal throughout your process. The Ho is that they are equal, the Ha will be they are not. The test results will give you a p-value. The Means are considered the same as long as p-value is greater than 0.05. Thus, you accept your Ho. Similar to the Test for Equal Variances previously, the results depict a top view of a bell curve (so you see a line) for each of the sample sets. At the center of each line is a dot representing the Mean for that data set. You want the dots from each of the lines to be aligned so to demonstrate the Means are the same.

25.5.2 Mood Median for Non-normal data

If you have non-normal data, then you will be looking to see if the Medians of each of your data sets is the same. The Ho is that they are equal, the Ha will be they are not. The test results will give you a p-value. The Medians are considered the same as long as p-value is greater than 0.05. Thus, you accept your Ho. It also calculates the overall Median for your process which you can compare to your target to see how off centered you are in your bell curve.

In conclusion, you want to come out of these hypothesis tests knowing that your process has the same Variance and Mean or Median regardless when you select your data source for testing. It also gives you the amount of variation your process has and how off you are from your target with respect to the Mean or Median.

Chapter 26: Problem Solving

We can actually classify a problem in one of three types. In some cases, the problem may encompass a couple of these types:

1. The first type is when the standard is not achieved. I.e. you are targeting less than 5% scrap and you consistently have 8%; or the customer is requesting 95% on-time delivery of all components and the most your group has gone to date is 93%.
2. The second is when you are meeting the standard, but the customer changes it on you, moving up the bar. I.e. your company is competing for a contract with the military and they decide that 95% on-time delivery is not good enough, they expect the winner of the contract to be able to accomplish 98%.
3. The third is when you are meeting the standard sometimes. I.e. in a week, your drilling machine is meeting the customer's specifications on Monday and Tuesday, but on Wednesday it barely makes the spec's, Thursday it misses it by 6% and Friday you are back meeting the spec's.

Now think of a standard as your target or requirement, what your customer is wanting you to achieve. Are you doing a DMAIC project because you are not reaching the target? Or you are reaching it inconsistently? Or you were meeting the requirement without an issue until customer changed the requirement on you. If we take the Improve Customer Responsiveness Project as the example, the customer service representatives are responding to the customer requests in less than 8 hours sometimes, similar to type 3. Digging into the defectives which are the types of requests, we see that this occurs only with two types. With the other three types, we notice we completely miss the boat and never make it back in less than 8 hours, making it more of a type 1.

In a nutshell, your problem will be tied to one of these three types. It's important you figure out which one, so it'll help you focus on the right solutions. The 8-Step process in Problem Solving:

1. Make sure your problem is clearly understood

2. When you have a big problem, break it down in pieces

3. Set a standard (i.e. target)

4. Conduct RCA to understand the causes of your problem

5. Develop action log

6. Test the actions

7. Evaluate the results

8. Take action if the Test result is:

    a. Successful: Standardize

    b. Not successful: go back to the RCA (step 4)

26.1 PDCA

With introduction of Improvement Phase, you will have your hypothesis based on your solutioning. This is a good time to introduce PDCA: Plan-Do-Check-Act in this chapter. This acronym means:

- **P**lan: Propose a hypothesis/theory

- **D**o: Pilot your hypothesis/theory

- **C**heck: Compare results to see if hypothesis/theory is correct

- **A**ct: Depends on the check

    - results match, create the standard, train and launch

    - results do not match, adjust hypothesis/theory and re-pilot

In a Traditional company, if we were to depict how PDCA is conducted in percentages, it would be similar to:

10% Plan
50% Do
35% Check
5% Act

What this shows is the classic "get it done!!" expression many use in meetings when they find out something is broken or not working. Unfortunately, it drives the wrong behavior. Everyone gets right into putting in place possible solutions they just came up with on the spot without vetting them. When little planning is done, you spend most of your time in a circular Do-Check activity. It's similar to trial and error. You put the first solution you find in place hoping it will solve the problem. If it does, then you are lucky. Most of the time it does not.

The expression "go back to the drawing board" is what an LSS person would tell them. Spending time in the planning phase figuring out exactly what the problem is, root causing and only then coming up with possible solutions to test is the way to go. You may spend more time here, but it will cut time in the other phases, so a typical PDCA shown in percentages would look like:

40% Plan
20% Do
20% Check
20% Act

26.2 DMAIC segmented into PDCA and the Problem-Solving Steps

Guess how many of the eight problem solving steps are in the PLAN piece of the PDCA? The first five! The remaining three cover the DO, CHECK, and ACT. Now think of the DMAIC framework you are using in this journey, how many of the methods and tools have you used during the PLAN piece?

We are going to look at the eight problem solving steps from the standpoint of your entire lean six sigma journey. Using the DMAIC framework you are covering these tools in the different phases....let's see some of the tools in your toolkit that actually covered each step of the PDCA as shown below.

PLAN – includes steps 1 through 5

Step 1: Make sure your problem is clearly understood:
- SIPOC
- VoC
- Charter
- Pre-Mortem / FMEA
- Gemba
- Spaghetti Diagram
- VSM Current State

Step 2: When you have a big problem, break it down in pieces
- Pareto
- QFD
- CTQ Drill down tree

Step 3: Set a standard (i.e. target)
- Project Capability

- Performance Standards

Step 4: Conduct RCA to understand the causes of your problem
- 5 Why's
- So, What's
- What If's
- Fishbone causes
- Hypothesis testing

Step 5: Develop action log
- Fishbone – possible solutions
- FMEA – controls to decrease failure mode
- VSM future state

DO – includes step 6: Test the actions
- Piloting actions from Action log
- Kaizens
- 5S

CHECK - includes step 7: Evaluate the results
- Comparing project capabilities
- SPC
- Control charting

ACT - includes step 8: Test is successful: Standardize
- Implementation Plan
- Deployment Strategy
- Lessons Learned

The idea is that you can problem solve by starting with a problem statement and using the 8 steps or using PDCA or going through a full DMAIC project. The key here is to know when to do which. And that comes from applying the tools you have learned and seeing whether they helped you solve the problem at hand. The more improvement projects you execute, the more you will find you can solve the problem by applying the toolkit you have learned.

IMPROVE PHASE

Finally, we move from understanding the problem thoroughly to finding solutions. This is where the magic happens.

Let us take the doctor example: you now know how bad the situation is. Here is where you get the remedy to get better.

Chapter 27: Fishbone – Finding Possible Solutions

You recall in Chapter 21 you listed all of your possible causes affecting your problem statement on a Fishbone diagram. That concluded the end of the Analysis phase.
Now you are in the Improve phase which is solutioning your causes. Don't forget that besides brainstorming with your team possible solutions, you can rely on the eight steps in problem solving and root cause methods as well.

The idea is to get with your team, go through each of the causes, and replace the cause by a possible solution you have come up with. If we take the Improve Customer Responsiveness project, "Need training on request types' steps" is one of the causes. After brainstorming, a possible solution is to create a "How To" for the top request types. It's easier to list this possible solution as an action in the Action log. Go to Appendix B to see an example table for the Action log.

Once the team completes the exercise, you will have a list of possible solutions. In some cases, you will note that one solution can cover multiple causes on your Fishbone. As a sanity test, go through each of the possible solutions and see if it will impact your problem statement.

Implement	Prioritization Key	Impact	
		High	Low
	Easy	1	2
	Hard	3	4

The only issue you may face when conducting this exercise is the many possible solutions you have come up with. Which one do you do first? Some solutions may not even fall within your department so how can you get those accomplished? The way to not feel overwhelm is to prioritize your possible solutions with the prioritization key you see here. Based on the solution you have, see if it is easy or hard to implement and by implementing it, will it have a high or low impact on your problem statement.

To guide you on this prioritization key, we'll take the Improve Customer Responsiveness project as an example and prioritize some of its possible solutions:

- "How To" for the top request types: the team feels this will be relatively easy to do and will be a high impact because it's going to standardize how the customer service representatives work. Priority: 1.

- Create Standard Work: will not be high for impact because we noticed that statistically the customer service representatives were doing things the same way. It's going to be easy to put in place, but the impact will be low. Priority: 2.
- Get a single point of contact technician: the team feels this will not be easy at all because we need to get the manager from another department to buy-in on this solution. But if we had this, we would go faster with our technical questions, so the impact is high. Priority: 3.
- See if IT can create a patch for the systems: this was answering the cause "MRP & ERP information differ." The team feels that it will be hard to put in place since they need to put in a request and see if budgeting will allow it. At the same time, it won't impact the problem statement as much because it only occurs 10% of the time. Priority: 4.

Once you have completed prioritizing your actions, you should decide which you plan to go forward with in this project and pilot. These actions will be recorded on your action log only once, so any solution with multiple causes should still be placed as one solution in the action log.

The ones that are prioritized as easy to implement and high impact should be the first on your action log to test. If you feel that the ones that are easy but have lower impact won't take much of your time, then you can place them on your action log. Don't discard the hard to implement with high impact, you may be able to put together a plan with your team on how to get it done. If this is the case, place them on your action log. The ones that are hard to implement and have low impact should be put on hold for now. Concentrate on testing the easy and high first.

Now that you have consolidated all of the solutions and create an action log which listing by priority the actions, use the Prioritized Action Log template to fill them out. With the Action column in, you can start putting together your PDCA steps for each of the solutions:

Plan: Remember to spend the time planning how you will be testing this action
Do: Once you have everything set up, write out the steps you need to do to
Check: place the target, standard, specification or requirement you are validating to ensure the action is a good solution for your project.
Act: if the action proves to be a solution for your improved process, make sure it is recorded somewhere (i.e. part of your improved process, a new standard in your quality system, etc.)

Remember, you have a good grasp of tools you can use to help you, use them! The idea is to see if you can do multiple pilots, relying on the solutions which were prioritized as 1's, 3's and 2's. This way you are certain to tackle your problem statement.

Chapter 28: 5S plus Safety

When it comes to Lean, the safety of people always comes first. This is why 5S has the addition of Safety. Some companies have now adopted 6S instead of "5S plus Safety" approach. Both designations are valid.

5S plus Safety is a Lean concept established in Japan and later adopted by the rest of the world. What is amazing is that the Japanese words all begin with "S" (with exception of Safety) and when translated, so do the English words. This concept is used to organize or declutter an area. Whether it's your office space or on the manufacturing floor.

Here is what it is made up of:

ANZEN – Safety: Ensure the area is void of danger and can be used to conduct the 5S. Examples:
- No wires, cords, plugs are obstructing the area
- No crane carrying objects above the area
- All equipment is anchored to the ground or adjacent wall. You don't want to start conducting a 5S on the factory floor and have pieces of heavy equipment not secured.

SEIRI – Sort: Separate what is needed from all items, discarding the unneeded. Examples:
- Closet: think of your closet, take out the clothes and place in three piles: clothes you wear, those you want to throw away and those you can give to charity.
- Inbox: think of your Outlook inbox where you have kept all of the emails that have cone in since you started your job, deleting very little. You will now need to go through each email to see if it's something you can delete, an email to keep, or an email to file into a folder for documentation.

SEITON – Straighten: Arrange the items in an easy-to-use manner. Examples:
- Closet: organize the clothes you are keeping by season or color or type
- Inbox: group the emails you are keeping by project name or customer name or another naming conversion that makes it easy for you to use

SEISO – Sweeping: Clean the items that are to be used so only the items required are present. Examples:
- Closet: go back to your empty closet and clean the area before you begin to place the clothes back in.

- Inbox: clean your inbox by reading the emails and placing them in the correct folders you set up. Delete the ones you do not need.

SEIKETSU – Standardize: Organize the items setting them up in order. Examples:
- Closet: you decided to have your clothes by type, start placing them back into the closet. i.e. the pants together, shirts together, etc.
- Inbox: you decide that you keep in your inbox only incoming that you have not read or actioned upon.

SHITSUKE – Sustain: Discipline, perform the first four S's to keep the area to the standard on a regular basis. In order to keep yourself organized and not fall back into chaos, make sure you have a routine set up.
- Closet: every time you wash your clothes, you will put them away in the same grouping by type
- Inbox: All emails that come in, you read, and action quickly then get either deleted or stored in a folder.

The main reason why we would conduct a 5S plus Safety is because it's the best householding tool in Lean which is virtually cost-free yielding great benefits. Once you organize the area, then you can see through all the clutter and use your eye of waste to identify any other possible TIM WOODS types of waste. A good example is when you believe you need more space on the factory floor but management refuses. Then you next recourse is to stay as is or to conduct a 5S plus Safety. Chances are you will see that reorganizing the floor will yield you benefits.

If you are interested in seeing an Office Manager before and after 5S, go to this YouTube video from CITEC Business Solutions back in 2012: http://www.youtube.com/watch?v=4PSw8Eq6JZM

In conclusion, Lean suggests you start with 5S plus Safety whenever you are wanting to tackle an issue. In some cases, this may be all you need to solve the issue. If not, you will need it as visual management so you can use TIM WOODS' eye to discover the wastes. Think of it this method as another visual way, similar to spaghetti diagrams and VSM. In a nutshell, 5S plus Safety is the first tool you should consider using whenever you believe there is chaos within your problem.

Chapter 29: Kaizen

Kaizen is a term that means to change for the better. It's a continuous improvement tool that can be used for an individual or group environments. To Steps flow as follows:

1. **Current Process**: We start with a process we want to improve. IMPORTANT: An ad-hoc way of working where everyone is doing their own thing is not a process. Therefore, if there is no consistent process the employees use, we cannot do a kaizen. We go to the Gemba and establish the current process. We see the breakdowns or wastes in the process, also called kaizen bursts. Kaizen bursts are quick and dirty improvements you find that can be tackled in a short period of time.
2. **Brainstorm Ideas**: We brainstorm possible solutions for these kaizen bursts.
3. **Pilot your ideas (PDCA)**: We test the possible solutions to see if they work out the way we planned.
4. **Communicate ideas**: If the solution is a success, we communicate to others in your group.
5. **Create Future State**: Next, we decide on incorporating it to the process, establishing a future state.
6. **Document**: We document it as a standard
7. **Train**: We teach all involved with this new process
8. **Becomes the new current process**: It now goes back to step 1 where this future state becomes the current state process.

Unfortunately, in many cases, the communication is not done. People do trial and error to get a better way of working but are scared to let others know of the improvement. This means the improvement never gets documented and others are not trained. This is what occurs in a traditional company where continuous improvement is more of checking the box than part of their DNA. Many employees do have the continuous improvement mindset, but with the red tape involved to get their ideas documented and implemented, they decide to improve their own way of working without making it a standard for the company. Of course, the company loses out, especially when this employee leaves.

IMPORTANT NOTE: There is also another way of laying out the Kaizen circle. You may have a future state in mind, basically, how you think the process should be. In this case you still follow steps 1 and 2. Instead of going to step 3 of solutioning, you go to step 6 where you establish your future state. Then you go through step 3 of brainstorming the solutions, step 4 and step 5. You can tweak the future state based on your results and go to steps 7, 8 and 9. In some cases, this process change works better because you are only taking care of the Kaizen bursts that will stop from having your ideal future state. There can be Kaizen bursts you identified which no longer matter because the process does not need it.

One of the dangers of using Kaizen is applying them to everything and shortcutting the DMAIC methodology. Kaizen work when the root cause is obvious and there is a good possibility of implementing a solution quickly. A Kaizen is usually focused on fixing one thing. Kaizens may be useful in the Improve phase of DMAIC in order to get solutions identified and implemented quickly. It also helps with PDCA testing.

So far, we have been talking about a kaizen as conducting continuous improvement to an existing process by focusing on a certain piece of the process. This means working out with your project team the solutions using TIM WOODS and 5S methodologies. In many cases, there exist kaizen events which are different.

When we talk about a Kaizen event, these are usually planned, structured workshops led by a certified BB or MBB. They usually take from 2-5 days to complete. The process is well scoped in advanced and the people involved, which in many cases are cross-functional, are invited to the workshop. The focus is to reduce waste and remove defects or breakdowns in the process. Keep in mind, when conducting an event, you are not looking into the variation of the process which means you are using only Lean, not Lean Six Sigma.

Kaizen Events have the following characteristics:

- Are planned, structured process improvement efforts that last just a few days at most
- Process exists and can be either a documented standard or performed the same way by the employees but is not documented
- Scope is typically narrow, focused and deals with cross-functional issues
- The focus is typically on waste reduction or specific defect
- Team members are those who do the job and/or those empowered to make decisions
- Is typically part of an ongoing effort where multiple other events are planned

Regardless if you are conducting a kaizen event or a Kaizen quick hit type, you want to go to the Gemba, or walk the actual place. Next map out a VSM current state, then identify the gaps, brainstorm solutions, test them and finally put in place a future state. Does this sound familiar? Instead of conducting a Kaizen event, you are following the journey in this book to go through the DMAIC framework which do cover these steps (as we have seen in the problem-solving chapter. The main difference is that conducting a DMAIC, you are not only looking at wastes in your process, you are also looking at variation.

If we look at the differences between a Kaizen event and LSS project, you'll find that:

- Process: Can be the same for either a Kaizen event or a LSS project; but in some cases, a LSS project may end up looking into more than one process.
- Scope: The scope is narrow within a Kaizen while an LSS project starts broader giving the possibility to scope it with VoC.
- Root Cause: Kaizens usually know the root cause, so they don't waste the time figuring it out in the session while a LSS project starts with an unknown root cause.
- Duration required: An LSS project can go from 3 to 9 months while a Kaizen can be less than a week, usually the quick hits are done in a couple of hours.
- Philosophies: An LSS project looks at lean which are wastes in the process and six sigma which is the variation through statistical analysis within the process. Kaizens only look at the wastes.
- Team Commitment: The team is required for an LSS project for its entire journey but in a Kaizen, you need the people for a limited amount of time.

Quick hit Kaizens, which are the ones you are going to focus on in this book and on your LSS journey, are using the lean tools to help you identify the wastes in the process once your root causes are known through the fishbone, spaghetti diagram or VSM. Please note that if your problem statement could have been resolved by doing a Kaizen event, then it was never a viable LSS project to begin with. You are going to be:

Go to the Appendix B to get a sample quick hit Kaizen template. Along with this template you will see an example of one filled out using the Improve Customer Responsiveness project as an example. It's important to identify the MURA, MUDA or MURI wastes as well as the benefits this Kaizen change will yield for the company.

Chapter 30: VSM Future State

You are now at the point where you have tested some solutions through PDCA and think you are ready to map out your future improved process. Maybe you haven't completed your Let us recap what you have done so far. You have gone to the Gemba and collected your observations. With your Gemba results, you created the Current State VSM. You have identified areas of waste using VA/NVA. You may have also seen the waste by creating a Spaghetti diagram.

Next you have gone through root causing your problem statement, looking at variation within the current process, hypothesizing whether you could reach your ultimate target and learning problem-solving techniques including Kaizen. You should have started testing some of the possible solutions using PDCA.

You should be well equipped to start mapping out the Future state. As we discussed earlier with the Kaizen process steps, there are a couple of ways you can do this. You can go through all your Kaizen bursts, fix them and then remap the VSM. Or you can go directly into mapping your ideal future state. Then looking at which solutions will be incorporated and proceed with your PDCA action log accordingly.

The reason I want to give you the options of either completing your PDCA action log then mapping out the future state or start by mapping out your ideal future state then completing your PDCA action log is because I took an VSM course that opened my eyes. In this course, the instructor, Dirk Van Goubergen, told us that the majority of the people do option one. But the truth is, doing option two will save you time because you are basically mapping out only the fixes that apply to this future state. This means that some of the Kaizen bursts become a non-issue. Just to complete my experience in this VSM course, as a group, we had completed the current state VSM and identified ~38 Kaizen bursts. The following morning, we mapped out our ideal state following the guidelines and found that only 16 Kaizen bursts still applied! I'm not going to instruct you do one over the other approach. Both approaches work. I just wanted to share with you this eye-opening learning I had when I took the course.

We are simplifying VSM building in this book because it may be the first time you hear of it. Similar to the VSM course I took, there are a multitude of courses that focus only on VSM.

Regardless of the approach you decide to use, here are some of the basic guidelines you follow when you are putting together your future state. Think of this as a check list. Some are better used in manufacturing environments while others can also apply in the office environments as well. When you are putting together your future state, go through this list and ask yourself with your team, "does this technique make sense for our process?"

1. **Cellular manufacturing** is about grouping components and factory cells. A family of parts is created within a cell of machines. This usually removes or decreases the machine changeovers. Directly related to manufacturing. Ideally you want to have the equipment and cells arranged in a sequence, so it supports the 1-piece flow logic.

2. **Takt Time** is the customer demand rate at which the finished product is completed to meet the customer's demand. This is useful when looking at processes' continuous flow and workload leveling. The idea is to have every step in your process to be below or at the takt time so that you can deliver at customer's demand.

3. **Standard Work** is a simple concept that entails having the process documented at the necessary details so that each of the employees performing the same work is doing it consistently the same. This is key if you want to ensure you reach takt time, thus employee loading is leveled.

4. **Continuous flow** (or one-piece flow) is removing the batch mentality and moving the piece from one station to the next without delays. So instead of making 10 pieces at a time and then moving to the next station, you are completing one piece and moving it to the station.

5. **FIFO** is first in first out method complementing the continuous flow. Though this was created for the factory floor, the office environment has adopted this method. This is where the first request coming in is the first one tackled, so you have a sequence. There is no prioritization or selecting the one you want to do.

6. The pull system is also referred to the **JIT (Just in Time)** so you are only working on customer orders. Basically, you are responding to the customer giving them what they want when they want it and you keep little or no inventory internally. You buy once you have the customer's order in hand.

7. **Quick Changeover also called SMED** (single minute exchange of dies) deals with converting a machine's parameters to meet the new standard that the piece needs to go through. Basically, you are having less downtime to modify the parameters and thus keep to the customer's demand. Shigeo Shingo developed the 3-stage method that reducing the time to changeover the machine. Some of the benefits to have

SMED are reducing WIP & the lot sizes, improve machine or resource's utilization, holding less inventory to make it more efficient.

8. **EPEI or EPEx** is basically Every Part Every Interval that shows you how fast you can cycle through your products in the process. It's the frequency that the parts are produced in the process. This is usually targeted to be as small as possible in order to minimize inventory. It is dependent on the changeover times and the number of part numbers assigned to the equipment. Also, if you are making various parts at the same time and there is a breakdown, then your customers will receive partial order instead of nothing.

9. **Supermarket or Kanban** is more of a push system where based on customer demand, you schedule the need of certain products and keep inventory to ensure the customer demand is met. This is a cost not a saving method, so it usually used when you have a consistent flow of customer demand (i.e. the customer wants more than you can produce as a pull system). Or you are managing bottlenecks in your process to keep to the takt time, smoothing out the process flow. You take out from the supermarket what the customer needs and you replenish the supermarket for next time.

10. **Pacemaker** is used to help the leveling of the work, smooth the operation of the process so it addresses the customer's demand. You find the step in the process that sets the pace for the entire workstream. It helping to set the pace for the process.

11. **Poka Yoke or mistake proofing method** which prevents an employee from making a mistake by placing preventive built-in designs in the process. This is great for promoting accountability in the employees, usually relatively low effort or time consuming and eliminates any possible disruptions to the flow of the process. This can be done on a process by reviewing each step, determining if it's the source of the errors, eliminate or reduce the source of error with an error proof type process.

12. **Heijunka leveling also known as production leveling** is keeping all the steps in the process below the takt time. You align the customer's demand with your in-house production schedule, so you are better at monitoring any fluctuations (i.e. customer demand goes up or down).

13. **Pitch** is the amount of time needed in a production area to make a container of products. Many cases pitch is used along with the heijunka box. It is the amount of time required to schedule and take away from the pacemaker in case there is a breakdown.

14. **TPM** (Total Productive Maintenance) is a system for improving the overall equipment effectiveness (OEE) that includes the availability, performance and quality. Establish a strategy to create autonomous ownership of the employees for maintenance.

15. **5S + Safety**. We covered this earlier in this course and is a great problem solver when looking at streamlining the process for an improved flow in future state.

16. **RCA methods** (5 Why's, What if's and So What's) questioning each of the steps in the process and as a whole to improve the outcome in the future state.

17. **Visual indicators** or visual management is used so that everyone working can understand at a glance. It can be a communication cell, production analysis board or a standardized work chart.

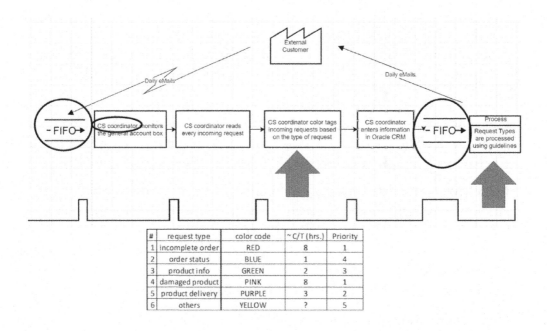

#	request type	color code	~ C/T (hrs.)	Priority
1	incomplete order	RED	8	1
2	order status	BLUE	1	4
3	product info	GREEN	2	3
4	damaged product	PINK	8	1
5	product delivery	PURPLE	3	2
6	others	YELLOW	?	5

Here is what was envisioned as the future state for the Improve Customer Responsiveness Project. Crazy easy, right?

Let us go through the techniques that were used from the list we just went through.

- A **FIFO** lane is placed on the emails coming in.
- There is a **one-piece continuous flow** until I hit the request types' process, then the one-piece flow will be within each of the request's sub-process

- A dedicated customer service representative is placed to monitor and dispatch the various types of requests. To put this in place we will need to **5S** the request folders. This can be considered a **pacemaker** placed at the start of my process.
- We have the coordinator color coding the requests so that we can spot them quickly using **visual management**.
- Instead of looking at all the requests the same, we are targeting the defectives (i.e. types of requests) and going to streamline every possible request type. Now this may be crazy for a start because the requests are more than a dozen. But if you recall, we did a pareto to filter out the main request types. We have decided as a team we will focus on these five types first, giving us the best bang for our buck! For these types we plan to put in place **streamlined** processes and create **standard work**.
- Though the overall process is continuous flow and FIFO, at the point where the requests are color-coded is not. Here we plan to create a **Kanban system** where estimated cycle time is known for each request's sub-process. Unfortunately, we cannot meet the customer's turnaround time for all the request types at this stage, but we will for certain types.
- Finally, to help with the Kanban system and customer's turnaround time, we will cross-train each of the customer service representatives. Based on the color codes, the priority is to take the longer lead time items first within the request types.
- In this perfect world, the customer is not going to the customer service representatives directly by sending an email. This change will be hard since customers are not bound to follow protocol. We plan to give them a templated email they can use by just filling in the blanks and sending, it will make it easier for both of us. Here we are creating a **poka yoke or mistake proofing** for the customer as well as creating **standard work** in a form of a template as well as guidelines for the customers. The selling point to the customers will be, if they use this template email, it'll go to the right place and will be taken care of sooner than any ad-hoc emails.

These improvements and new process all need to be tested through the PDCA. Once completed, it will be ready for implementation.

Chapter 31: Improvement Strategy

This chapter will deal with translating all of your findings from LSS language into your company language. First, let us recap what you have done so far:

- ✓ You have your ***problem statement*** in your Charter.
- ✓ You went through the analysis phase using Minitab® for stats along with visual tools (i.e. Gemba and VSM)
- ✓ You got some possible solutions to your problem statement when you conducted the fishbone diagram, VSM, and hypothesis testing

Now you are ready to put all of this information in a clear, concise and orderly fashion in order to present your ideas to your management and get approval to do some piloting on your solutions.

If you recall from the history explained back at the beginning of your journey, Walter Shewhart created the "Shewhart cycle" in the 1950's, which is known today as PDCA. PDCA stands for Plan-Do-Check-Act. We went through in more detail back in section 26.1. Similar to the eight-problem solving technique, think of the DMA from the DMAIC framework being your Plan, where you understand your problem statement. Now in the Improve phase, you are taking the proposed solutions, getting agreement at work to be able to test and see if they will be incorporated within your final improved process. You conduct the pilot for a given solution, check if it works. Incorporate it to your improved process if it does show improvement of the process, putting it in place by acting on it. If on the other hand, it does not yield the results you were hoping for, you may want to root cause the reasons why, see if it would be possible to tweak it and then go through the PDCA again, only if desired.

Data and facts are the main ingredients to this improvement strategy. This entails creating a safe environment where you can test your solutions in a systematic way. The aim is to optimize your process performance. Remember you have prioritized the list of possible solutions.

Now all you need to do is convert the solutions that do pass the check into benefits. This means in your Action log spreadsheet you will be adding two columns called "Benefit type" and "Benefit recorded". Here you are going to be placing which type of benefit you tackled as well as what it yielded for your project when you piloted.

Keep in mind this slogan: "Project success is directly related to the benefits it produces; Benefits can be quantitative or qualitative."

Below you will find a laundry list of benefits that can materialize in your project when you test successfully a solution. A benefit can be qualitative or quantitative. Your project should be reaping all the benefits from what you and your team were able to accomplish:

Qualitative Benefits

- Align to Strategy
- Bring value & appreciation to customers (i.e. letter, email, call)
- Cultural shift
- Develop Employees & Teams
- Morale (i.e. happy employees, rewards & recognition, perception)
- Preventative measures (i.e. avoiding increasing price, cost avoidance)
- Simplification
- Standardization

Quantitative Benefits (savings can be calculated and documented)

- Cash Flow
- Cost Reduction
- Customer Impact (i.e. Responsiveness; NPS survey; OTD-respect takt time; Strengthen relationship & grow business)
- Incremental Revenue
- Margin Enhancement
- Productivity
- Quality Improvements (reduce/remove Defects)
- Workforce Efficiency (reducing cycle time)

We are going to go through each benefit type in the following two chapters. Keep in mind, when talking to your management, benefits will help you enable your project's value. These benefits are what you will reap when you incorporate them into your final improved process.

Chapter 32: Qualitative Benefits

It is important to show the impacts your improved process will have on the company. We will begin by going through each of the qualitative benefits in this section so that you can have a better understanding of what each entail.

32.1 Customer Impact

Can be either as something that will bring value to the customer or the customer sends their appreciation on the improvement. You can achieve this for your project if you keep the Customer informed and possibly involved in your improvements, so they are aware of what is happening.

Examples of possible impacts your project has on the customer:

- Create and maintain loyalty
- Use diagrams to illustrate complex concepts
- Solve customer's issues
- Examples: how you know the Customer sends their appreciation is by:
  - Receive a letter, email, or call
  - Customer awards or recognition

32.2 Cultural shift

Occurs on your project when using change management methods to alter the paradigm at your company. I love using some of "The Toyota Way - 14 Principles" that you can find on Wikipedia using this link: https://en.wikipedia.org/wiki/The_Toyota_Way
The best way to know if this paradigm shift occurs is to give you examples describing the "From - To":

- *From* focusing on short term results *to* focusing on long term results and looking at trending. Improvements do not occur overnight and sometimes management gets absorbed with quarterly results, they forget about the big picture, which is where they want to be ultimately.

- *From* brushing incidents under the carpet and not discussing the problems *to* being open to report any incident. Only when you know there is a problem can you begin to improve.
- *From* empowerment given to a few people of the inner circle *to* empowering at all levels to make decisions on behalf of the company based on their expertise.
- *From* Silo base thinking *to* working together as a team to improve for the greater good
- *From* thinking change is bad *to* continuous improvement or change is good
- *From* having robots in the company that don't think, just do *to* everyone challenging the status quo to improve

32.3 Develop Employees

Employee development is all about enhancing the skill set of employees, so you have the right person with the right skill set in the right job. This ties closely to the morale because an employee doing something, they love will definitely be happier than someone who is not. This is where management needs to play a key role. Here are some examples:

- Managers need to get the employees involved in improvement initiatives. This creates inclusiveness and promotes engagement not to mention it also makes it easier for change management when deploying the solutions.
- Managers need to understand their employee's roles & responsibilities and more importantly, make sure the employee knows where they are in the entire organization. You want to create commitment and accountability on what they are to do, not on things that do not pertain to their expertise.
- Managers should have an employee training plan tied to career path so the employee knows what they need to do to move up the ladder and thus will establish loyalty.

32.4 Employees Morale

As just mentioned above, morale tied closely to the development of the employee. If an employee knows what their standard work is, applies their expertise and receives compensation in form of appreciation and/or recognition, you will have a content employee. What you do not want is to have employees that are talking at the watercooler about possible company closures or lay-offs. All this does is create chaos making the employees insecure and less productive. They are spending their time trying to find out whether they still have a job instead of doing the job. This includes any type of reorganization within the company as well. Some examples are:

- Employees do not want to be doing things that do not matter. They are hired for one reason and are now doing something completely different to fill a company's gap.
- They have a problem or a pet peeve that stops them from being content at work. You work with them to remove the issue, making their lives easier. Chances are they will help you next time you are struggling.
- Being valued, just like customers, is important to an employee's morale. You can give them visibility in forms of having them present to Leadership or having them lead a section of the project.

32.5 Preventive measures

Taking preventive measures occurs whenever you put in place any type of mistake proofing to ensure that costs which we are occurring in the old process do not in the new. You may turn this qualitative benefit to quantitative by estimating the savings logically and getting agreement from your finance group. Therefore, the qualitative benefit is that you know there was an impact and people are feeling it, but you cannot show it in numbers; the quantitative benefit is you can back it up with a dollar amount. Some examples are:

- Avoiding increasing price, cost avoidance
- Negotiating a contract without any liquidated damages
- Preventing the product's failure so warranty will not be used
- Improve procedures for field technicians
- Avoiding scrap or rework costs on new products
- Level loading commissioning engineers

32.6 Simplification

Is when you take something that is complex and simplify it, so everyone understands it. Some examples of what you can simplify in your project are the:

- Process
- Documentation (i.e. Manuals, instructions, procedures, etc.)
- Roles & Responsibilities

In many cases, you are going to be simplifying by utilizing:
- TIM WOODS Waste
- 5S + safety improvement

32.7 Standardization

Similar to simplification, standardization is a benefit most of your projects will have if you document, the process going forward and all pertinent employees are following this new improved process. Since you are putting together a deployment and implementation strategy, there is a high possibility you will have this as a benefit. It is hard to quantify how a standard process can lead to qualification benefits. Having said that, I have seen how standardizing helped improve productivity, reduce wasteful costs and / or improving workforce efficiency.

Chapter 33: Quantitative Benefits

Now we are going to go through possible benefits you can put a numeric value to.

33.1 Align to the Strategy of your business

This occurs when you work on a project, which is a sub-set of the company's bigger picture. For example:

- You align with your company's Hoshin plan or End-to-End transformation. If you are aligning with your companies' strategy, then you are working towards improving some key performance indicator or metric. i.e. on-time delivery needs to be consistent at 95% or better.
- You are looking at the financials or your operational plan. You put together a project that will identify the root cause for variance from expectations and solution how you can get back on target.

33.2 Cash flow

When it comes to cash flow or fund flow, you will need to determine with finance if you want it to be a one-time reduction savings or incremental with a specific timeframe. The main types of projects are targeting receivables, payables or inventory fund flow. Some examples are:

- Accounts Receivable issues:
  - o Past dues: payments that are late from the customers. You improve the process so that you reduce the delinquency.
  - o Contract language: place in proposals language where you are to receive money earlier or milestone-based, instead of receiving it at the end of the contract.
- Managing accounts payable is all about paying out at the right time and possibly at a set time. You can standardize when to payout, reducing the number of transactions done at multiple times within a month. This will also yield productivity.
- Inventory funds flow is a big issue with many factories. Having more materials in hand than what you need to satisfy the customers' demand is just wasted cash. Some examples are:

o Figuring out what raw materials to buy and store is the key. Just in time (JIT) is a way of decreasing inventories and you can calculate your savings by making wiser decisions on the make-buy in procurement.
o Having agreements with some suppliers where you will continually receive materials, creating a supermarket in your factory. Therefore, looking into your receiving process and ensuring that you are not allowing any materials earlier than required by the production lines will decrease your inventory.
o Improving your turnover of materials by effective material planning
o Reducing your inventory of finished goods by creating a discount for your distributors or customers, so you do not scrap the obsolete merchandise.

33.3 Cost Reduction

Cost reduction is on every corporation's mind. Remember, LSS is not about reducing headcount but working more efficiently. This means working on more value-added tasks for the customers. So, it's about working smarter, not harder!

A past instructor had shared a Toyota story that stuck with me. When the car industry was down, Toyota did not ask for any government bail-out money and more importantly, they did not lay anyone off. They cut the overtime and bonus. But instead of laying off Toyota divided their employees into 3 groups: 1 group continued working in production of cars, 1 group was sent for training or higher education, and last group was set out to help communities. After 6 months, the car industry was still down, so Toyota just swapped the groups...the ones who worked went to training, the ones trained go out to the community and the ones that were helping the community when back to work. When this down slide ended, Toyota didn't have to rehire or retrain. They just got all their people back to work. And this built loyalty! Keep this story in mind when you are doing cost out projects.

In addition, DO NOT forget that the quality of the work is not to suffer. Cutting corners as a result of cutting any quality measures is going to make the costs go up once the problem reaches the customer. Basically, you have just created the 1-10-100 defect rule from chapter 16. Finally, cutting costs in your department and passing it on to another department will not be a benefit, for it's not an improvement but a deferral of work.

For valid cost reduction savings in your project, start by making sure you have a baseline amount incurred before the PDCA improvements are done. Then once you go through the PDCA and record your findings, you will see that the possible cost benefits, whether you incur a reduction to the baseline amount or eliminate it completely. Here are some examples:
• Warranty: when you have some part that keeps on failing on the field and you figure out how to avoid it. Putting the new process in place will eliminate these site failings, hence a cost reduction for the company.

- Scrap or Rework reduction: you know your actual baseline costs spent, let's say they are $25K/month; improvements in the process show only $5K/month. Therefore, you have an 80% improvement, $20K/month cost savings.
- Materials: let's say you change engineering designs to make the product more reliable, now it requires less material, i.e. need 15 instead of 50 sheets of steel to create the bin. Savings are $200K/month and 70% improvement. You can also go to a different material that is less in cost but as good as the original material in quality which will also yield savings.
- Purchasing / Procurement: having more than one supplier will keep costs competitive; savings would be between the vendors' bidding. Or you sign an agreement with a vendor to keep the costs for the materials the same for an amount of time. A great example is steel or aluminum. The price fluctuates and getting a fixed price will decrease your chances of paying more when the prices go up.

33.4 Customer Impact

Customer impact can be qualitative, as you learned in the previous chapter or quantitative. Quantitative means that you may save your customer money by helping them with their problems, showing advantages to alternatives or improving the relationship between your company and the customer. This is creating a win-win situation with you and your customer. Let's look at some of the examples:

- Customized design or retrofit: for example your custom fit the bin to the customers tower, managing the engineering hours so they did not surpass the customer's expectation of 50 hrs. (Actuals were 46 hrs.)
- On-time delivery (respect takt time): agree with customer on standard delivery schedule as product gets produced to ensure you keep to their commitments
- Strengthen relationship & grow business: for example, you signed $100M order after working together to streamlining the fulfillment process on both sides
- Responsiveness: for example, being able to respond to customer demand faster, like the example project we have been using in this book (going from ~16 hrs. to ~4 hrs. of responding to customer requests, yielding 75% decrease)

33.5 Incremental Revenue

Incremental Revenue occurs when your project improvements yield permanent sales revenue through increase price or volume. This does not mean you just raise the price because in today's market, to be competitive, most of the time you are decreasing the price and cutting costs internally in order to make the shareholders happy. Let us look at the examples:

- Value-based price: you upgrade your existing product and/or rebrand it. Basically, you are increasing the price due to significant branding. At this point, your product brings customers value and is priced accordingly.
- Create a new market demand with your design
- Volume: get in more revenue when increasing the volume selling by giving a discount; your margin will decrease but your sales will increase reducing inventory.
- Samples: have the customers experience your product or service as a trial before they purchase it. This gets customers on the fence to try it out at no expense from their end and it gets your product/service in their hands.

33.6 Margin Enhancement

Margin Enhancement deals with decreasing your costs, increasing your price, managing down risks / claims or changing the scope so that the calculated margin is greater than what it was originally. Some examples are:

- Managing scope changes in a project: the scope changed where customer is now buying spares or requesting additional work done. At this point, chances are you are going to charge a price which exceeds the original margin. For example, the margin for the spares is at 64% versus the overall project is valued at 22%. Your overall margin ends up going up by 3-4 points in the margin by selling the spares.
- Make or Buy Decisions: you may find that outsourcing has become expensive, especially when you only have one supplier, so you look at bringing the work inhouse. If bringing the work back into your company is feasible, you can see an incremental revenue where making the product because of the costs of making it has gone down.
- Reducing Risk, Claims or Back charges: through improving your product or service's quality you find less warranty money going towards replacements or fixes. Or establishing a contingency fund for your project during execution and then liquidating it at the end when it is not used.
- Lump sum agreement: deciding to sell your services for a fixed price. For example, instead of charging by hour for on-site work, you charge for the service itself. It them takes less than the allotted time to make the fix onsite, you increase your margin because your actual costs are less than they were foreseen at the start of the work.

33.7 Productivity

Productivity is another benefit your company may thrive for, but the truth be told, it should be something every employee should too. As we spoke earlier about headcount, LSS is not about headcount reduction.

- Many companies take their time replacing people that leave or retire, adding pressures to existing employees. Employees that work smarter with shorter timeframes versus those who work longer hours produce better work and are less stressed. In many cases, with today's global way of working, we are always on, never disconnecting. I've conducted one too many workshops where the goal was to get employees back to working their 40 hours per week instead of more. This is why productivity is closely tied with morale and work-life balance that is a struggle in many corporations today.

- Removing redundant or wasted tasks in an employees' standard work improves productivity. It gives them either time back as we just discussed or gives them the opportunity to work on things, they are interested in but have not had the chance to. For example, an engineering group was always late with their new products because they spent most of their time correcting existing products. Once the quality was improved with the existing products, they could go focus on new product development.

- Many companies have issues growing because they reach a point where they can't keep up with the customer demand. Improving productivity is key.

- Manufacturing: if your project is in the factory, think of reducing changeover time on a machine, or increasing the parts going through the equipment before the changeover occurs.

- Office: a couple of simple office examples are reorganizing the space in the office so that the people working together are closer; or taking out the IT improvement of placing a printer per floor – where they think they saved the money on the number of printer and maintenance plan but forget all the time wasted in productivity by employees having to walk to the printer and wait for their stuff

33.8 Quality Improvements

Quality Improvements is reducing or removing defect(s) to a process that is out of control and restoring it to the desired parameters. Some examples are:

- Decrease the company's Cost of Quality: Many companies will have the replacement of product due to failure part of Cost of Quality. Working on a project to avoid failures to occur on customer site can significantly decrease costs. Or if you are in a factory setting, you will look at your equipment's performance and consistently monitoring with statistical charts to ensure calibration.

- People safety: Have you ever walked on a construction or mining plant? Many of them are proud of their number one quality metric – people. In fact, they show the number of days without injuries.
- Implementations that involved improving the quality of people, tools, processes, products and/or services would be a quality improvement. i.e. ISO or TQM; or quality of life at work which leads to retention.

CONTROL PHASE

The last and important phase for your improvement. Here is where you make sure that all the hard work you have done translates to an adopted standard practice for your workplace.

Let us take the doctor example: in order to avoid going back to the doctor, you will make changes to your lifestyle and stick with them!

Chapter 34: Statistical Process Control (SPC)

When we think of control mechanisms, we think of three main methods:

1. Risk management – AVOINDING POTENTIAL FAILURES which you have been monitoring throughout your project in the FMEA tool. Many companies underestimate the power this tool can be when used correctly. It is used for preventing failure or being proactive during the life if a project. If you prevented a failure from occurring, then you have automatically saved time and money for the company.

2. Mistake Proofing or poka-yoke (meaning fool proof) – AVOIDING AND MONITORING FOR POTENTIAL FAILURES and helps maintain the solution by ensuring that a mistake is not made and passed on to the next station or department to handle. You want to allow quality at the source. This means that individuals are responsible for the quality of their work and do not pass on a defect, like they would say "throw it over the fence". The employees in this situation actually stop the line and fix the issue.

3. Statistic Process Controls – MONITORING REALTIME FOR POTENTIAL FAILURES using control charts to visually see if there is a problem with the process while it is executing. Statistical process controls or SPC are control charts that monitor the performance of the process over time.

Keep in mind, you have applied control mechanisms prior to the Control Phase. Do you recall the FMEA, X-bar and I-bar charts? Now that you have reached the final phase of DMAIC, you are going to put in place the Control charts you believe will help the people who are operating the process to see potential failures. You are passing the torch so that it is the employees responsible to execute on the process are the ones that will be monitor for any potential failures, putting in place preventative measures.

One important takeaway is that you and your project team should not be babysitting this process once you close the project. Buy-in from your stakeholders, process owner and executors of this improved process is essential. The Control phase is going to establish the process control plan, deployment plan and the statistical process controls so you can give the employees following the process the means and ownership required.

SPC charts were invented by Dr. Walter Shewhart in the 1920s while working in a telephone factory. Instead of having the operators stop the line every time they believed there was an error, he gave then charts to see if the error was just random or a real problem. This way, stopping the line was not expensive and only occurred when it was needed.

You have done a great job at prioritizing your solutions and going through the PDCA to pilot them. Now in the Control Phase, SPC is what we use to control the future state process. SPC will guide you, telling you whether you should get involved to change the process or leave the process alone. The SPC charts will also show whether your process is in control or out of control. This is the focus of process variation and it can be broken down into two parts: common or special causes.

- Common causes: are described to occur by chance and are random while the process is running as designed. This is considered stable. Some examples are getting a new piece of equipment that should be set up properly but isn't or a person forgetting to do a step in the process correctly and does it slightly differently. If these common causes occur, then the process itself has not been touch and we consider it IN CONTROL. This means you don't change anything with the process, but you do make changes around the process so that it is properly used.

- Special causes: occur when something non-random happens, a disruption or sporadic results are being felt by the process. Examples can be broken tools, calibration issues, equipment stalled or jammed, or an untrained person running the process. If this occurs, then your process is out of control and you need to place corrective actions. You do this by looking at what changed have occurred that impact the process and brainstorms solutions.

If you are still unsure what the two type are, let me give you a day to day example.

Common Cause: When you drive to work, you always take the same route. Sometimes it takes you 27 min, sometimes 34 min depending on the traffic lights and traffic. The difference in times based on the traffic is considered as common cause, therefore you're not going to change the route.

Special Cause: But if you find out that there is construction or an accident on your route, then you plan to take the backroads to get to work because if you take your daily route it will take you an hour to get to work. This is considered a special cause.
Control charts are used to monitor the process over time and can help you see the performance of your process.

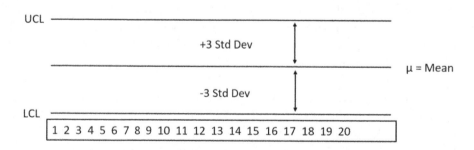

The chart will always have a middle line which is the mean, then it will give you the upper control limit (UCL) and lower control limit (LCL) which are calculated by taking the average of the data and applying a plus and minus three standard deviations from the mean. These are called the performance characteristics. Now do not get this confused with specification limits. SPC have nothing to do with the specification limits. Think of SPC as the voice of the process and will show you how it is performing over time.

Here are some of the SPC control charts:

- **X Bar Chart**: view the mean and variability of the process between multiple operators over time

- **Individual Chart**: views the mean and variability of the process with one operator and looks at stability of your data over time

- **R Chart**: shows the range of the data over time

- **Moving Range Chart**: Monitors the mean of your process and the variation

We have already seen in details of the charts above in the Analyze phase and should not be a surprise for you. Remember the X-bar was used if you had multiple operators or appraisers while the I-bar was used if you had only one operator. Both showed you if your process was stable and tested the variation in the process. The R Chart was found in your capability analysis showing you the range of the data over time. The only new chart in the list is the MR Chart. This will show you the moving data monitoring the mean of your process and the variation.

These SPC charts are used to monitor your process so do not think of them as a one-off. You should consider using them as part of your controls when your project is closed out, implemented and the improved process is being used. Therefore, think of these charts when putting together your process control plan so that the employees working the process can use to control the process.

Using the SPC correctly means you need to understand when a common or special cause can occur. You want to prevent unnecessary process adjustments, just like the saying goes "do not fix what is not broken."

Here are the control charts' rules, how do you know if your data, hence your process is out of control? The eight general rules are:

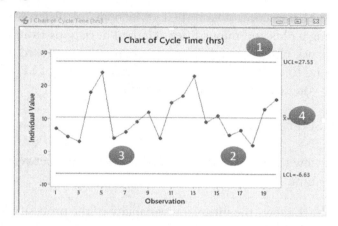

1.   A point is outside the upper or lower control limits…this means a data point is beyond the red lines

2.   9 consecutive points are on one side of the mean…you can see in my case I had 4 data points at most, not 9

3.   6 points in a row, either increasing or decreasing…you can see in my case I had 3 data points, not 9

4.   14 points in a row alternating up and down…you can clearly see my chart does not zig zag from point to point, thus my process and measurement system is in control.

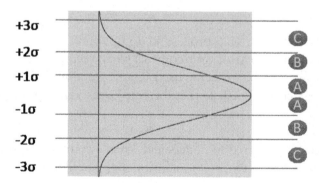

5.   15 points in a row in area A, above or below the center line

6.   8 points in a row beyond area A, above or below the center line

7.   4 out of 5 points in a row in area B or beyond

8.   2 out of 3 points in a row in area C or beyond

34.1 I-MR Chart

This is the only chart from the SPC charts you have not produced to date, and it is used to monitor the Mean and variation of your process. Go to Appendix A to see the step-to-step instructions of the report. This report holds:

- the I-Chart for individual observations of your process which give you the Mean.
- The Moving Range chart that gives you the Variance to your process.

This is the perfect report to run using the data from your future state which include your PDCA improvements.

When you interpret your results, start by looking at each of the two charts to make sure you are in control. If either of the charts depicts out of control, then your improved process is in trouble. Your PDCA actions were not enough to stabilize your process, so you need to go back into the Improve phase and root cause this occurrence.

Once you know your process is in control, then you can look at the Mean from the I-chart. It should be better than it was back in the current state. In fact, you should have met your target or come very close. Basically, you are meeting the CTQs you set out to satisfy by improving the process. The Variance can be compared with your current state as well but just going back to your original Descriptive Statistics report and getting the variance there. A lower variance tells you that your improvements did statistically move the bar when it comes to variation in your process.

For example, at the end of the Improve Customer Responsiveness project, the I-MR charts show in control. The Mean has gone from the 10.45 hours to ~4 hours. The variation which originally 43.6 hours span is now ~ 2 hours which is amazing.

Chapter 35: Statistical Future Results

Just as we just compared the current process to the future process running the I-MR chart in the previous chapter, here we are to run the same reports we did back in the Measure and Analyze phases to see if we actually improved. Therefore, as soon as all your PDCA testing is completed, you are to run the following reports:

- **Descriptive Statistics**: check to see if you are now Precise with your improved process
- **X-bar or use the I-bar from I-MR chart**: how is your accuracy for your process now with respect to what it was in the current state?
- **Capability Report**: check to see where if your sigma value went up and your DPMO value went down. Also look at the bell curve, has the shape improved? Is the spread less wide? are you stable with your process? Are you now centered with your target? How are your performance capability indicators?

If you want to, you can also rerun your Gage R&R and the hypothesis tests to get a sense of your accomplishments. At this point you and your team want to see statistically how you tackled the variation of your process.

Chapter 36: Implementation Plan

Let us look at what an implementation plan will consist of:

- Action Plan
- Process Control Plan
- Communication Plan
- Training Plan
- Quality Plan

We have already gone through the Action Plan in a previous chapter and you have learned how to create it along with the benefits.

When it comes to the Process Control Plan, Communication Plan and Training Plan, we will go through them in this chapter.

Finally, there is a quality plan which is usually specific for each company. Some are ISO certified and have a designated quality management system for their company, others keep departmental documents. Because the quality system is unique for each one of you, depending where you work, we will not be discussing quality management systems in this book. It is expected that you follow the one at your workplace and ensure that your process along with any documentation required at your site are completed so you do not lose all the hard work you put in realizing this project. The best way to ensure you do not forget is to include it in your Action Plan. Go to Appendix B for the Action Plan sample template.

36.1 Process Control Plan

You are closing your project, updating your quality system with documentation that describes the new way of working. But without any monitoring, how do you know it's being used properly?

This plan incorporates the requirements or the specification for your CTQs which are your tolerances, and their control methods. Keep in mind, the best control methods are the visual ones because you can quickly see where you are at and how you are trending. Of course, numbers are usually complementing the charts. Eventually, the objective is to place your controls into an establish scorecard or dashboard for everyone to view and start a discussion.

We are going to start with baby steps, putting together the charts that are meaningful for your project. In a previous chapter, we went through SPC charts. Think about which SPC charts could be part of your control plan; would your SPC charts help in mistake proofing systems and what you plan to place as your standard operating procedures so that the monitoring of your improvements is seamless.

Besides SPC, go back to your FMEA tool. The reason why it was a live tool throughout this project is because it's final output of current controls you placed is what you should have in your control plan. Everything you have been doing in this journey is inter-connected. Your final FMEA for this project should have the controls you are going to use in your control plan to monitor the process when it goes live.

Go to Appendix B to find a Control Plan template you can use to list what should be used for monitoring your process. The template is simple and incorporates the following columns:

- Control: what is the title or subject you are wanting the future operators to control
- Unit of Measure: the unit used to measure this control
- Target / Spec's range: the range or target measurement the control needs to adhere to
- Frequency: how often should this control be checked to ensure control…need timely feedback
- Method: how are you going to measure
- Control Owner: who is going to be executing this measurement control

Now some control plans also include columns like last recorded date & time, FAQs, corrective actions (CA), CA owner, CA date & time. It's usually up to your company's quality management system how the control plan is going to be documented and executed. The idea here is to monitor the process in order to ensure it stays in control.

36.2 Communication Plan

I'm sure you have seen communication plans before if you've been on projects or managed a project. In Lean Six Sigma's implementation plan, it is used for the same reason. To list out what deliverable you are planning to communicate, when are you going to communicate it, how is it going to be communicated, who is doing the communicating and who is receiving the information. Now what you are going to be communicating is your project improvements and the controls you put in place. You want to make sure that all your good work is going to be taken seriously by your peers and management.

Go to Appendix B to find a Communication Plan template you can use which is simple and incorporates the following columns:

- Communication: what type of communication is this? What do you want them to know?
- Description: what are the details of this communication? What does it entail?
- Technique: how are you planning to communicate this to them? By phone, webinar, teleconference, newsletter, email, in person, etc.
- Timing: when are you planning on communicating your project improvements with them
- Owner: who is going to be communicating the message? Can be yourself or someone on your team
- Recipients: who is your target audience for this communication?

36.3 Training Plan

When you are getting ready to launch your improved process, you want to make sure that the right people are trained. During your PDCA pilots, you may have had some people part of the testing to see if it was feasible. This is great for adoption and you can actually have them help you in the training. Keep in mind that scheduling one training may not be enough. In some cases, you may not have everyone attend. In other cases, they were there but the time between the training and them using the process was long, so they forgot what they learned. Thus, refresher trainings as well as open-door policy to having them reach to you (or your team) to help them through this period is important.

When putting together your training plan, keep in mind the different audiences you will have. You will need to cater your training to the audience. For example, if you are training management or leadership the message is usually at a higher level than when you are training the individuals that will be part of the process.
Go to Appendix B to find a Training Plan template you can use which is simple and incorporates the following columns:

- Topic: what are you going to train them on? What is the title of the training?
- Description: what are the details of this training? What does it entail?
- Technique: how are you planning to train them? By phone, webinar, teleconference, newsletter, email, in person, etc.
- Timing: when are you planning on conducting this training
- Trainer: who is the person training the topic?
- Recipients: who is your target audience for this training?

Chapter 37: Deployment Strategy

Many confuse the difference between the implementation plan and a deployment strategy. In fact, the plan is part of the strategy. If we were to look at it as steps to take:

    a. We start by putting in place the process control plan.

    b. Next, we put an implementation plan together. Don't forget this includes updating your quality system with the appropriate documentation required so your improvements are recorded.

Everything is now documented properly, you have set up how you want to communicate it to your company, you know which controls need to be monitored and who you will be training.

    c. Now you need to strategize how you are going to do this, basically how are launching your new process? And most importantly, how will it stick, meaning the improved process is going to be used. This is your deployment plan. A quick way of putting together a strategy plan is doing it as a timeline. You can also do it in a Table, Matrix or another type of framework. The idea is to lay out the blueprint on how you are going to roll out your project to make sure it gets effectively used going forward in your workplace.

The key for your strategy is that it will be adopted at your workplace and become the current process until there is another project to improve it again in the future. This is the full circle the process will go through when you have a continuous improvement mentality. Right now, you need to think of change management. How to encourage the people to use your improved process. For this book, you will do a simplified version of change management using the steps above.

Go to Appendix B to find a couple of examples of the deployment strategy plans.

Chapter 38: Customer Satisfaction

So how much did you involve your customer in your project? Here are some important questions to answer when looking at satisfying your customers:

    a. Was the Customer informed at the beginning of this project?
    b. Was the Customer involved during the execution of this project?
    c. Was the Customer part of the PDCA piloting?
    d. Now you are at the end of your project, how will you communicate to your Customer the changes?
    e. How do you measure customer success going forward?

Let us take each one and see possible answers:

    a. Was your Customer informed at the beginning of this project? Keep in mind, you were asked to go to your customers for their CTQs, you should all answer Yes to this question.

- Yes: This is a great way to maintain change management and increase the adoption rate.
- No: This means that you want to see if the improvement works before you get them involved. Is an option but not the best technique to use for change management.

    b. Was the Customer involved during the execution of this project? And
    c. Was the Customer part of the PDCA piloting?

- Yes: Establishing a solid relationship, easier for change management process and creating a partnership.
- No: This means that you want to do it yourself, just in case it doesn't work and so you do not get anyone else spending time on it. Yet you lose the team thinking, the creation of any type of relationship and it will be hard to change their way of working since they were not involved…they may come up with some ideas once you close your project having to reopen it.

d. Now you are at the end of your project, how will you communicate to your Customer the changes?

- INVOLVED: Part of the team, Customer Impact Benefits and Customer involved in the Control Plan
- NOT INVOLVED: Email communication, Newsletter, Marketing materials or do nothing. Just remember that if you decide to do nothing, you will never know for sure if your customers are satisfied…it's all going to be your perception.

e. How do you measure customer success going forward?

- Net Promoter Score (NPS): started by Harvard Business and is widely used in many corporations when sending out surveys to external customers. The general question asked is "How likely would you recommend XYZ company to your colleagues?" The customers answer the question by selecting a number from 1 to 10. The response is a Promoter (9-10), Neutral (7-8) and Detractor (1-6). Basically, the calculation to get your percentage is (Promoter – Detractor)/Total sum.
- Surveying: is different because it is usually a series of questions you ask the customer not just one.
- Benchmarking: is a process of identifying best practices, comparing your own practices to it and adapting the appropriate best practice to your own process.
- Setting up a Metric: creating a quantitative measure that is usually placed in a dashboard, scorecard or comm cell. This is a way of tracking and monitoring your process by measuring its output.

There are also other ways of achieving customer satisfaction. For LSS, the important matter is that you do. What are you going to do?

Chapter 39: Lessons Learned

"The past is where you learn the lesson, the future is where you apply the lesson...Don't give up in the middle!" **Anonymous**
"Those who do not remember the past are condemned to repeat it." **George Santayana**

39.1 After Action Reviews

We are going to look at two ways of recording your project's lessons learned. The first is called AAR or After-Action Review. It's a structured approach to reflect what just happened and can be done either formally recording the information or informally by just having a conversation. It was first introduced by the military used for combat missions.

The AAR is composed of responding to the following:

- What went well or strengths of the occurrence?
- What did not go as well or what weaknesses were exposed?
- What are the areas of improvement if you were to conduct the same event again?

What's great about the AAR is that you can do it anywhere. Whether you decided to do it in a meeting setting or just walking out of meeting, conducting it with a colleague while walking back to the office. Some of the characteristics are:

- Everyone can do it
- Honest and Open discussion
- Focus on the results
- Brainstorm ways sustaining what worked and keep doing it
- Develop recommendations for overcoming obstacles

The process of the AAR is as stated above, responding to three questions after the event has occurred:

- What went well?
- What should we avoid doing next time?
- What do you recommend for future projects?

39.2 Project Lessons Learned

Lessons Learned (LL) are recorded with enough detailed of anything that significantly stood out during your project. You have gain knowledge during this journey, experienced the things that went well and those that were obstacles in your path of success. Understanding what went right and what went wrong builds on your experience in executing LSS projects. Chances are you will remember what didn't work and try not to repeat it. But if too much time passes between projects, how do you make sure you don't forget?

One of my learning experiences was that sometimes you forget things in a project that has a long duration. I managed a consortium project which lasted two years. And when we sat down as a team, we talked about the big things that impacted out project margin. It wasn't until we sat with the customer to conduct a LL that we heard of other things that occurred which they considered impactful, but we did not consider in our internal LL. Worse there was a whole incidence that did impact us on cash flow and we totally forgot to record it! My lesson learned from conducting these lessons learned meetings was that when I am responsible for a long duration project, I should cut it up into phases or sections to conduct the LL so it's still fresh in everyone's minds. Go to Appendix B for a sample of a LL template pertaining to an LSS project.

Some of the key characteristics of LL which differs from AARs are:

- Dedicated meeting organized for the event
- Formally documented
- Database or repository for future endeavors
- Covers all aspects of the life cycle

Both AAR and LL follow the same ground rules:

- No wrong answer
- Open to new ideas, be Creative
- Every person's view is accepted and regarded as value
- No figure pointing
- Consensus where possible
- Ensure active participation

Summary

I hope you have gone through this book, used it as a manual and improved a process at work. Going through process improvements the first time may be daunting so simplifying it with a simple recipe should have you thinking about waste and variation in a positive light. The improved process you have today will become your current process. As time passes and circumstances change, there is a good chance you will take today's process and enhance again.

As a final note, if you have captured lessons learned while using this book, and are willing to share, please forward them to the following email azconsulting13@yahoo.com or leave your comments on my website: www.azconsulting-sp.com. I take all feedback seriously and it helps me improve my materials. We are in fact talking about LSS so continuous improvement should be for all!

APPENDIX A: Minitab® Statistical Software Step-by-Step

Descriptive Statistics

Data Source looks like....

CS rep	Cycle Time (hrs)
Lisa	7
Lisa	4.5
Lisa	3
Lisa	18
Lisa	24
Lisa	4
Lisa	6
Lisa	9
Lisa	12
Lisa	4
Lisa	15
Lisa	17
Lisa	23
Lisa	9
Lisa	11
Lisa	5
Lisa	6.5
Lisa	2
Lisa	13
Lisa	16

Go into Minitab® to initiate report...

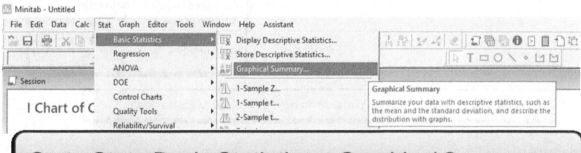

Go to Stat> Basic Statistics > Graphical Summary...

Filling out the required fields...

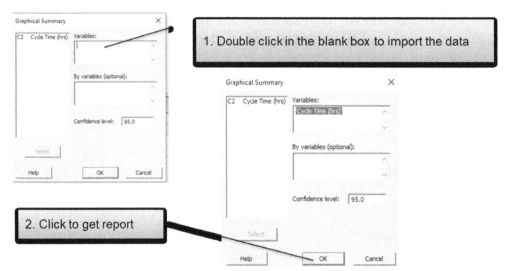

1. Double click in the blank box to import the data

2. Click to get report

Interpreting Descriptive Statistics report...

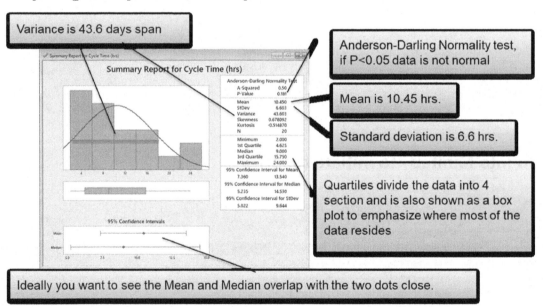

Variance is 43.6 days span

Anderson-Darling Normality test, if P<0.05 data is not normal

Mean is 10.45 hrs.

Standard deviation is 6.6 hrs.

Quartiles divide the data into 4 section and is also shown as a box plot to emphasize where most of the data resides

Ideally you want to see the Mean and Median overlap with the two dots close.

I-Bar Chart

Data Source looks like....

CS rep	Cycle Time (hrs)
Lisa	7
Lisa	4.5
Lisa	3
Lisa	18
Lisa	24
Lisa	4
Lisa	6
Lisa	9
Lisa	12
Lisa	4
Lisa	15
Lisa	17
Lisa	23
Lisa	9
Lisa	11
Lisa	5
Lisa	6.5
Lisa	2
Lisa	13
Lisa	16

Go into Minitab® to initiate report...

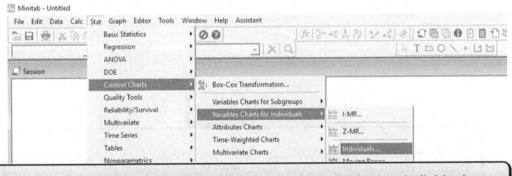

Go to Stat> Control Charts > Variables Charts for Individuals > Individuals...

Filling out the required fields...

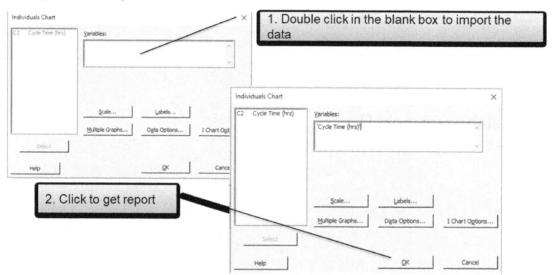

1. Double click in the blank box to import the data

2. Click to get report

Interpreting Control Chart...

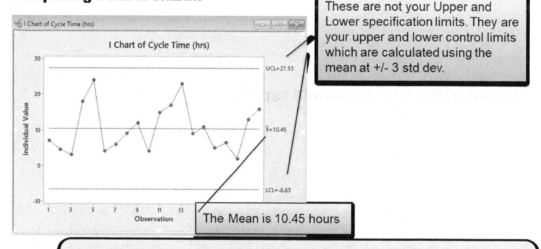

These are not your Upper and Lower specification limits. They are your upper and lower control limits which are calculated using the mean at +/- 3 std dev.

The Mean is 10.45 hours

Process is in Control. Minitab will color code dot(s) in RED if process is found to be Out of Control. See Chapter 34 for the Control Charts Guidelines.

X-Bar Chart

CS rep	Cycle Time (hrs)
Lisa	7
Lisa	4.5
Lisa	3
Lisa	18
Lisa	24
Lisa	4
Lisa	6
Lisa	9
Lisa	12
Lisa	4
Lisa	15
Lisa	17
Lisa	23
Lisa	9
Lisa	11
Lisa	5
Lisa	6.5
Lisa	2
Lisa	13
Lisa	16

Data Source looks like....

Go into Minitab® to initiate report...

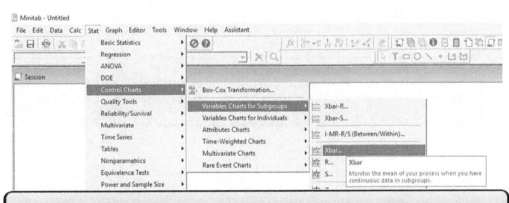

Go to Stat> Control Charts > Variables Charts for Subgroups > Xbar...

Filling out the required fields...

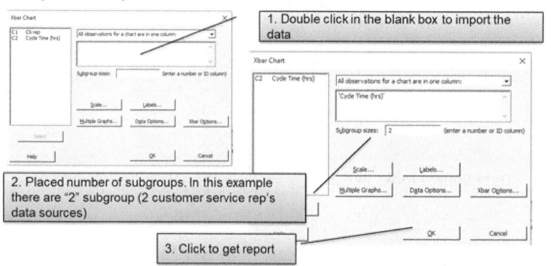

1. Double click in the blank box to import the data

2. Placed number of subgroups. In this example there are "2" subgroup (2 customer service rep's data sources)

3. Click to get report

Interpreting Control Chart...

These are not your Upper and Lower specification limits. They are your upper and lower control limits which are calculated using the mean at +/- 3 std dev.

The Mean is 10.45 hours

Process is in Control. Minitab will color code dot(s) in RED if process is found to be Out of Control. See Chapter 34 for the Control Charts Guidelines.

Gage R&R Study

Part	Operator	cycle time (hrs)
1	1	13
2	1	11
3	1	5
4	1	16
5	1	8
1	1	12
2	1	9
3	1	4
4	1	15
5	1	8
1	2	11
2	2	9
3	2	5
4	2	15
5	2	7
1	2	12
2	2	10
3	2	4
4	2	16
5	2	8

Data Source looks like....

#	request type	average
1	incomplete order	123
2	order status	99
3	product info	111
4	damaged product	34
5	product delivery	78

Go into Minitab® to initiate report...

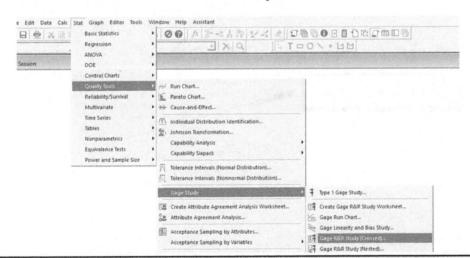

Go to Stat> Quality Tools > Gage Study > Gage R&R Study (Crossed)...

Filling out the required fields...

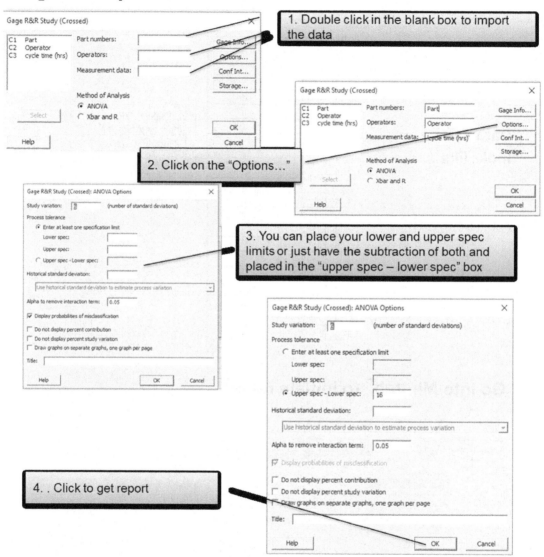

1. Double click in the blank box to import the data

2. Click on the "Options..."

3. You can place your lower and upper spec limits or just have the subtraction of both and placed in the "upper spec – lower spec" box

4. . Click to get report

Interpreting Gage R&R Crossed Type report...

You want to see low Gage R&R for repeatability and reproducibility, with a high part-to-part so that your MS has little variation error

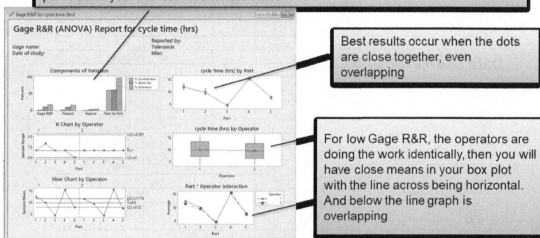

Best results occur when the dots are close together, even overlapping

For low Gage R&R, the operators are doing the work identically, then you will have close means in your box plot with the line across being horizontal. And below the line graph is overlapping

Gage R&R

Variance Components

Source	VarComp	%Contribution (of VarComp)
Total Gage R&R	0.5107	2.87
Repeatability	0.4786	2.69
Reproducibility	0.0321	0.18
Operator	0.0321	0.18
Part-To-Part	17.2741	97.13
Total Variation	17.7848	100.00

Process tolerance = 16

Total Gage R&R should be less than 10% of Variation, 10% to 30% may be acceptable. > 30% the MS is not accepted. In this example, it's 16.95% which is acceptable of the measurement system (MS). The main cause of variation is in the repeatability not reproducibility. Therefore they need to investigate training materials for the operators, so they are consistent in their responses as well as the process steps they take to respond.

Gage Evaluation

Source	StdDev (SD)	Study Var (6 × SD)	%Study Var (%SV)	%Tolerance (SV/Toler)
Total Gage R&R	0.71464	4.2879	16.95	26.80
Repeatability	0.69179	4.1507	16.40	25.94
Reproducibility	0.17928	1.0757	4.25	6.72
Operator	0.17928	1.0757	4.25	6.72
Part-To-Part	4.15621	24.9373	98.55	155.86
Total Variation	4.21721	25.3032	100.00	158.15

Number of Distinct Categories = 8

Gage R&R for cycle time (hrs)

Distinct categories is the MS' ability to detect the different characteristics. So this number is the non-overlapping confidence intervals of the process variation. Rule of Thumb:

< 2 distinct categories = MS has no value controlling the process because it cannot distinguish between data sets.

< 5 distinct categories = MS may not have enough resolution

> 5 distinct categories is ideal

Attribute Agreement Analysis Study

Data Source looks like....

Samples	Operator	cycle time (hrs)	CT <8?	Standards
1	1	13	Fail	Pass
2	1	11	Fail	Pass
3	1	5	Pass	Pass
4	1	16	Fail	Pass
5	1	8	Pass	Pass
1	1	12	Fail	Pass
2	1	9	Fail	Pass
3	1	4	Pass	Pass
4	1	15	Fail	Pass
5	1	8	Pass	Pass
1	2	11	Fail	Pass
2	2	9	Fail	Pass
3	2	5	Pass	Pass
4	2	15	Fail	Pass
5	2	7	Pass	Pass
1	2	12	Fail	Pass
2	2	10	Fail	Pass
3	2	4	Pass	Pass
4	2	16	Fail	Pass
5	2	8	Pass	Pass

Go into Minitab® to initiate report...

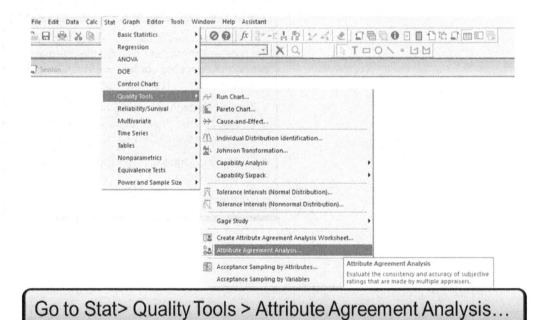

Go to Stat> Quality Tools > Attribute Agreement Analysis...

Filling out the required fields...

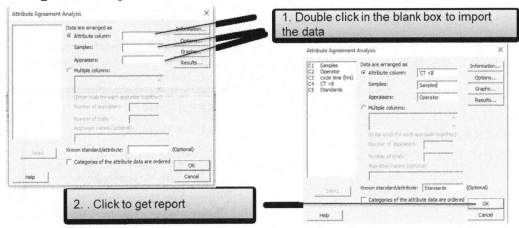

1. Double click in the blank box to import the data

2. . Click to get report

Interpreting Attribute Agreement Analysis Study...

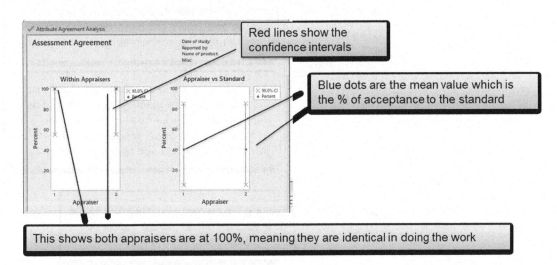

Red lines show the confidence intervals

Blue dots are the mean value which is the % of acceptance to the standard

This shows both appraisers are at 100%, meaning they are identical in doing the work

Interpreting Attribute Agreement Analysis Study...

Attribute Agreement Analysis for CT <8

Within Appraisers

Assessment Agreement

Appraiser	# Inspected	# Matched	Percent	95% CI
1	5	5	100.00	(54.93, 100.00)
2	5	5	100.00	(54.93, 100.00)

Matched: Appraiser agrees with him/herself across trials.

Fleiss' Kappa Statistics

Appraiser	Response	Kappa	SE Kappa	Z	P(vs > 0)
1	Fail	1	0.447214	2.23607	0.0127
	Pass	1	0.447214	2.23607	0.0127
2	Fail	1	0.447214	2.23607	0.0127
	Pass	1	0.447214	2.23607	0.0127

> Kappa shows the level of agreement. Closer to 1 means perfect agreement. Less than 1 means that the agreement alignment is being reached by chance.

> Kappa Rules:
> 0.9 – 1 Excellent
> 0.7 – 0.89 Good
> 0.5 – 0.69 Needs Improvement
> < 0.5 MS is in trouble

All Appraisers vs Standard

Assessment Agreement

# Inspected	# Matched	Percent	95% CI
5	2	40.00	(5.27, 85.34)

Matched: All appraisers' assessments agree with the known standard.

> This needs to be > 90% for the measurement system to be accepted. The agreement among appraisers is > 90% but with the standard it is not. Therefore, the 8 hours is a stretch goal and it's wise to rerun this report using a more reasonable target, i.e. 16 hours.

Fleiss' Kappa Statistics

Response	Kappa	SE Kappa	Z	P(vs > 0)
Fail	-0.428571	0.223607	-1.91663	0.9724
Pass	-0.428571	0.223607	-1.91663	0.9724

> NOTE: The Appraiser vs Standard does not pass when you are placing your standard as your goal and in your current process you are far from it. In this case, place your current goal in the standard and rerun the report.

Attribute Agreement Analysis

All Appraisers vs Standard

Assessment Agreement

# Inspected	# Matched	Percent	95% CI
10	9	90.00	(55.50, 99.75)

Matched: All appraisers' assessments agree with the known standard.

> Placing the current standard, the MS is now accepted with the assessment agreement being at 90%.

Capability Analysis Report

Continuous Data Source looks like....

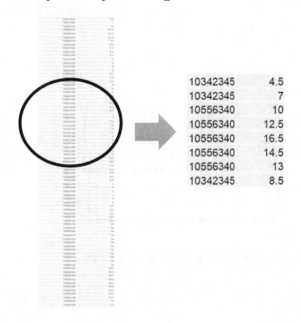

10342345	4.5
10342345	7
10556340	10
10556340	12.5
10556340	16.5
10556340	14.5
10556340	13
10342345	8.5

Go into Minitab® to initiate report…

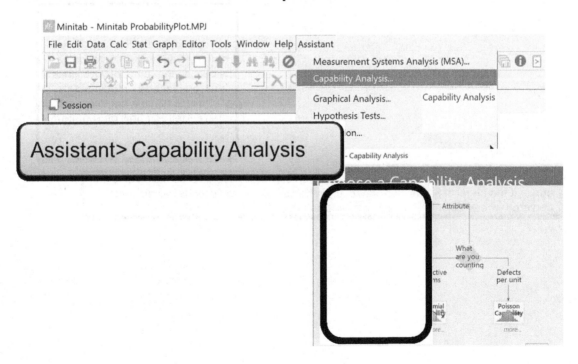

Assistant> Capability Analysis

Filling out the required fields...

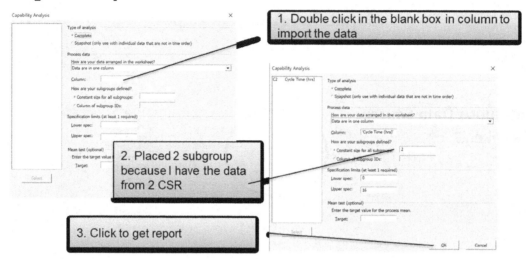

1. Double click in the blank box in column to import the data

2. Placed 2 subgroup because I have the data from 2 CSR

3. Click to get report

Interpreting Capability Analysis Report...

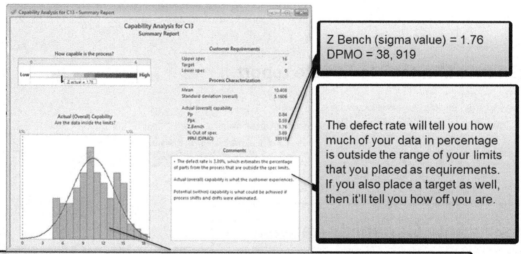

Z Bench (sigma value) = 1.76
DPMO = 38, 919

The defect rate will tell you how much of your data in percentage is outside the range of your limits that you placed as requirements. If you also place a target as well, then it'll tell you how off you are.

Based on the spec.'s limits placed as requirements, you can see data points outside the curve. If the target of 8 was also added, then the bell curve would look skewed or off-centered where majority of defects are outside the USL.

Interpreting Capability Analysis Report Cont'd...

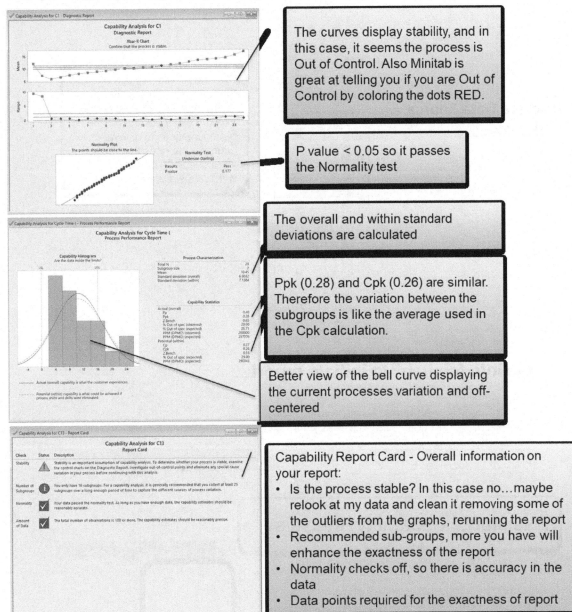

The curves display stability, and in this case, it seems the process is Out of Control. Also Minitab is great at telling you if you are Out of Control by coloring the dots RED.

P value < 0.05 so it passes the Normality test

The overall and within standard deviations are calculated

Ppk (0.28) and Cpk (0.26) are similar. Therefore the variation between the subgroups is like the average used in the Cpk calculation.

Better view of the bell curve displaying the current processes variation and off-centered

Capability Report Card - Overall information on your report:
- Is the process stable? In this case no...maybe relook at my data and clean it removing some of the outliers from the graphs, rerunning the report
- Recommended sub-groups, more you have will enhance the exactness of the report
- Normality checks off, so there is accuracy in the data
- Data points required for the exactness of report

Binomial Capability Report

Total Calls	defect >8 hr
250	25
257	27
260	27
256	27
259	28
259	22
250	21
260	30
254	24
253	27
251	15
254	20
251	24
256	31
255	22
249	21
257	22
252	21
258	20
252	30
251	24
256	31
255	22
249	21
257	22

Discrete Data Source looks like....

Five Defectives Types make up the Cycle time Defect. I know the number of calls that came in every day. I ask the customer representatives to give me their count for the ones that they were unable to respond to within the same day.

Go into Minitab® to initiate report...

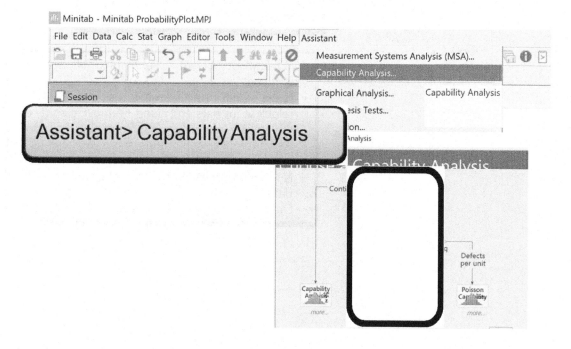

Assistant> Capability Analysis

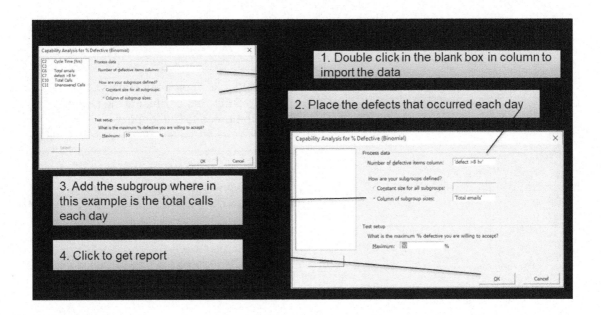

1. Double click in the blank box in column to import the data

2. Place the defects that occurred each day

3. Add the subgroup where in this example is the total calls each day

4. Click to get report

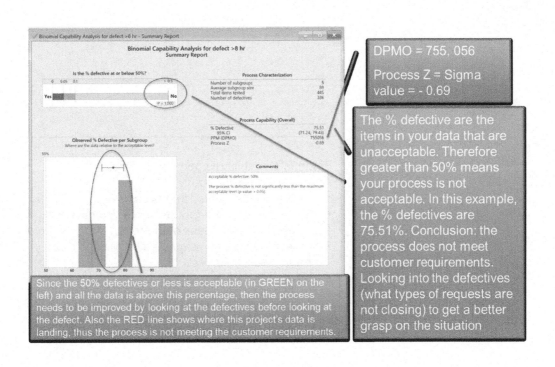

DPMO = 755, 056

Process Z = Sigma value = - 0.69

The % defective are the items in your data that are unacceptable. Therefore greater than 50% means your process is not acceptable. In this example, the % defectives are 75.51%. Conclusion: the process does not meet customer requirements. Looking into the defectives (what types of requests are not closing) to get a better grasp on the situation

Since the 50% defectives or less is acceptable (in GREEN on the left) and all the data is above this percentage, then the process needs to be improved by looking at the defectives before looking at the defect. Also the RED line shows where this project's data is landing, thus the process is not meeting the customer requirements.

Interpreting Binomial Capability Report Cont'd...

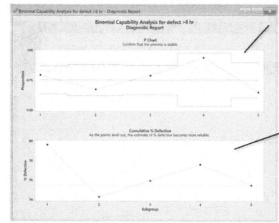

P chart looks at process stability. If there are no RED dots or outside the range, then the process is in control

Yet the % defectives are high…reducing the defectives will improve this graph

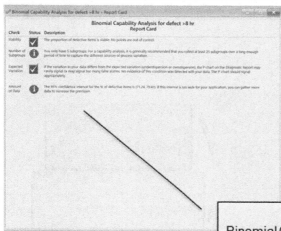

Binomial Capability Report Card - Overall information on your report:
- Is the process stable? In this case yes
- Recommended sub-groups, more you have will enhance the exactness of the report
- Is there the variation expected? If Minitab gives you a check, then yes.
- Data points required for the exactness of report

1-Sample t Test Report

Data Source required comes for Descriptive Statistics:

- **Mean = 10.45**
- **Std Dev = 6.603**

Go into Minitab® to initiate report...

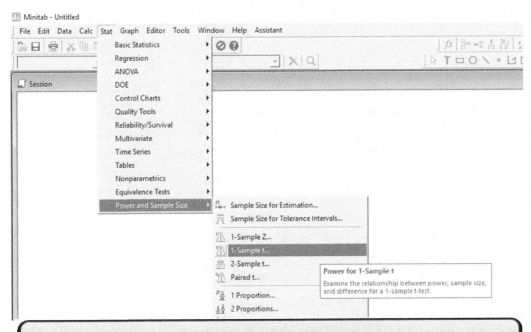

Stat > Power and Sample Size> 1-Sample t....

Filling out the required fields for SAMPLE SIZE...

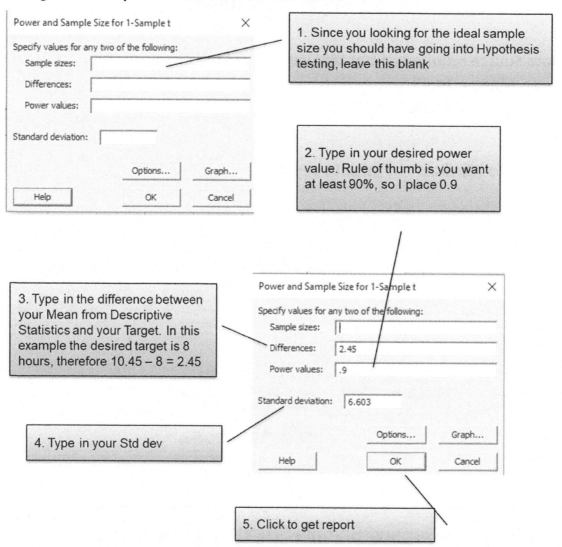

1. Since you looking for the ideal sample size you should have going into Hypothesis testing, leave this blank

2. Type in your desired power value. Rule of thumb is you want at least 90%, so I place 0.9

3. Type in the difference between your Mean from Descriptive Statistics and your Target. In this example the desired target is 8 hours, therefore 10.45 – 8 = 2.45

4. Type in your Std dev

5. Click to get report

Interpreting 1 Sample t Test – SAMPLE SIZE...

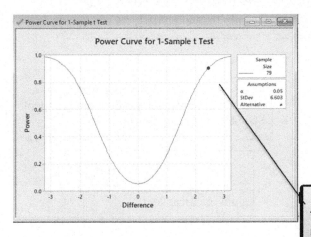

Power and Sample Size

1-Sample t Test
Testing mean = null (versus ≠ null)
Calculating power for mean = null + difference
α = 0.05 Assumed standard deviation = 6.603

Results

Difference	Sample Size	Target Power	Actual Power
2.45	79	0.9	0.902697

Power Curve for 1-Sample t Test

> This show that in order to have reliable results for hypothesis testing, we need at least 79 data points

Filling out the required fields for POWER VALUE...

Based on the 90% Power value, we need at least 79 data points...but we have only 14 so let's see how reliable the hypothesis will be...

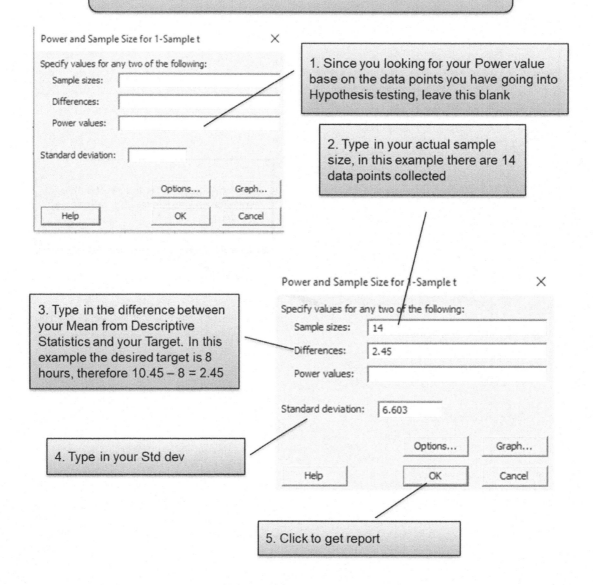

Power and Sample Size for 1-Sample t

Specify values for any two of the following:

Sample sizes:

Differences:

Power values:

Standard deviation:

Options...   Graph...

Help   OK   Cancel

1. Since you looking for your Power value base on the data points you have going into Hypothesis testing, leave this blank

2. Type in your actual sample size, in this example there are 14 data points collected

3. Type in the difference between your Mean from Descriptive Statistics and your Target. In this example the desired target is 8 hours, therefore 10.45 – 8 = 2.45

Power and Sample Size for 1-Sample t

Specify values for any two of the following:

Sample sizes: 14

Differences: 2.45

Power values:

Standard deviation: 6.603

Options...   Graph...

Help   OK   Cancel

4. Type in your Std dev

5. Click to get report

Interpreting 1 Sample t Test – POWER VALUE...

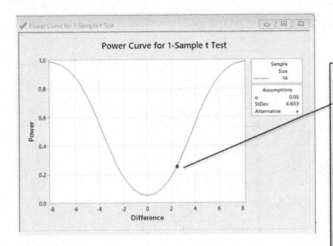

This show where the power value is located...below the results show that if we proceed conducting the hypothesis testing with 14 data points, the power in the results is going to be only 25%...not good. There is a 75% chance that the hypothesis testing results are going to be incorrect because the Beta error will manifest. The idea is to get more data!

Power and Sample Size

1-Sample t Test
Testing mean = null (versus ≠ null)
Calculating power for mean = null + difference
α = 0.05 Assumed standard deviation = 6.603

Results

Difference	Sample Size	Power
2.45	14	0.251055

Power Curve for 1-Sample t Test

1-Variance Report

Cycle Time (hrs)	
Lisa	Anna
7	9
4.5	10
3	9
11	9
13	11
4	5
6	6.5
9	2
12	13
4	11
6	7
7	8
5	5
8	10

Discrete Data Source looks like....

Go into Minitab® to initiate report...

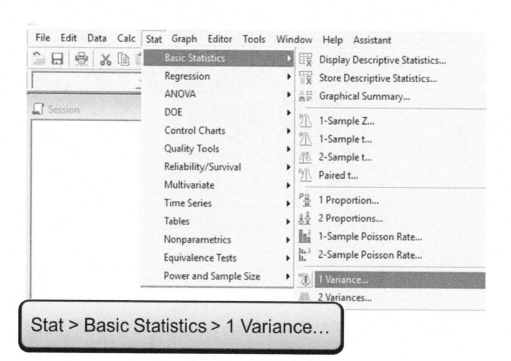

Stat > Basic Statistics > 1 Variance...

Filling out the required fields…

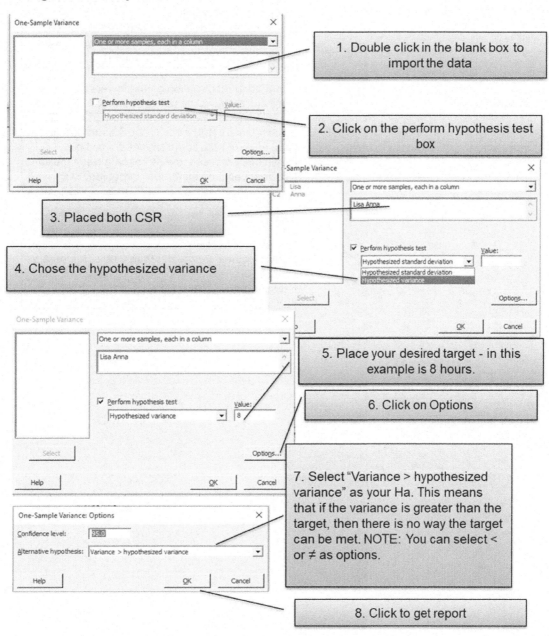

1. Double click in the blank box to import the data

2. Click on the perform hypothesis test box

3. Placed both CSR

4. Chose the hypothesized variance

5. Place your desired target - in this example is 8 hours.

6. Click on Options

7. Select "Variance > hypothesized variance" as your Ha. This means that if the variance is greater than the target, then there is no way the target can be met. NOTE: You can select < or ≠ as options.

8. Click to get report

Interpreting 1 Variance report...

◢ Test and CI for One Variance: Lisa, Anna

Method

σ: standard deviation of Lisa, Anna
The Bonett method is valid for any continuous distribution.
The chi-square method is valid only for the normal distribution.

> **Select correct results:**
> - Non-normal data, use the Bonett method
> - Normal, use the Chi-Square (in this example the data is normally distributed)

Descriptive Statistics

Variable	N	StDev	Variance	95% Lower Bound for σ using Bonett	95% Lower Bound for σ using Chi-Square
Lisa	14	3.14	9.85	2.36	2.39
Anna	14	2.91	8.49	2.12	2.22

> The standard deviation on the lower end of the bell curve shows the representatives ~ 2 hours.

> The variance is just above the 8 hours which is not so bad. With some changes, maybe in training or process, the representatives time can be reduced, and the 8-hour target reached

Test

Null hypothesis $H_0: \sigma^2 = 8$
Alternative hypothesis $H_1: \sigma^2 > 8$

Variable	Method	Test Statistic	DF	P-Value
Lisa	Bonett	—	—	0.256
	Chi-Square	16.01	13	0.249
Anna	Bonett	—	—	0.431
	Chi-Square	13.80	13	0.388

> Ho = variances are equal
> P < 0.05 reject Ho
> P> 0.05 accept Ho
> The p-values are greater than 0.05,. This means that both customer service representatives can respond in less than 8 hrs.

Test for Equal Variances Report

Cycle Time (hrs)	
Lisa	Anna
7	9
4.5	10
3	9
11	9
13	11
4	5
6	6.5
9	2
12	13
4	11
6	7
7	8
5	5
8	10

Discrete Data Source looks like....

Go into Minitab® to initiate report…

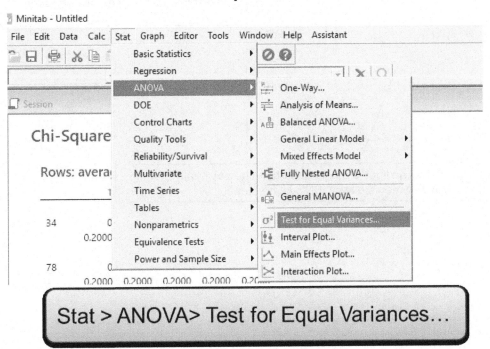

Stat > ANOVA> Test for Equal Variances…

Filling out the required fields...

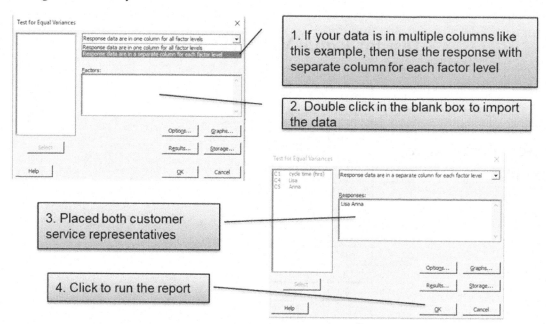

1. If your data is in multiple columns like this example, then use the response with separate column for each factor level

2. Double click in the blank box to import the data

3. Placed both customer service representatives

4. Click to run the report

Interpreting the Test for Equal Variance Report...

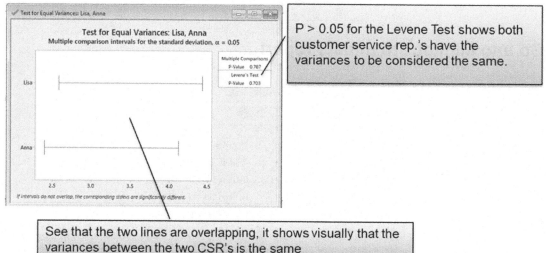

P > 0.05 for the Levene Test shows both customer service rep.'s have the variances to be considered the same.

See that the two lines are overlapping, it shows visually that the variances between the two CSR's is the same

ANOVA – Equal Means Report

Cycle Time (hrs)	
Lisa	Anna
7	9
4.5	10
3	9
11	9
13	11
4	5
6	6.5
9	2
12	13
4	11
6	7
7	8
5	5
8	10

**Data Source
looks like....**

Go into Minitab® to initiate report…

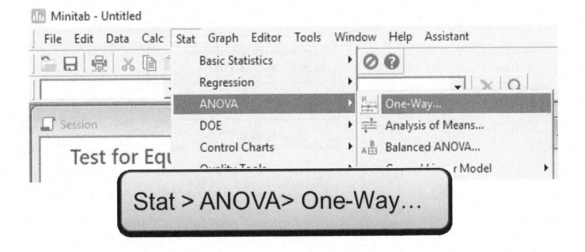

Stat > ANOVA> One-Way…

Filling out the required fields…

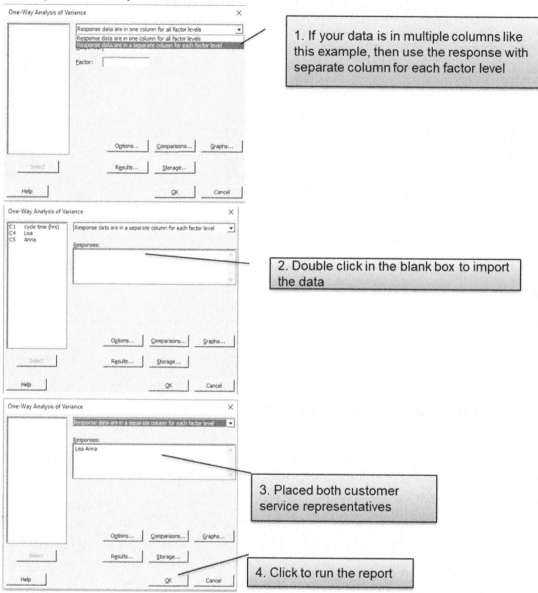

1. If your data is in multiple columns like this example, then use the response with separate column for each factor level

2. Double click in the blank box to import the data

3. Placed both customer service representatives

4. Click to run the report

Interpreting ANOVA – Equal Means…

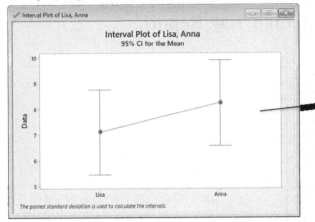

This is interval grouping which shows you that the two CSR's do overlap which is a good sign for the hypothesis Ho where the Means are the same.

One-way ANOVA: Lisa, Anna

Method

Null hypothesis	All means are equal
Alternative hypothesis	Not all means are equal
Significance level	$\alpha = 0.05$

Equal variances were assumed for the analysis.

Ho = all Means are equal
$P < 0.05$ reject Ho (means not equal)
$P > 0.05$ accept Ho

Factor Information

Factor	Levels	Values
Factor	2	Lisa, Anna

Analysis of Variance

Source	DF	Adj SS	Adj MS	F-Value	P-Value
Factor	1	9.143	9.143	1.00	0.327
Error	26	238.464	9.172		

This Means that the CSR's are responding to the requests the same way.

Model Summary

S	R-sq	R-sq(adj)	R-sq(pred)
3.02848	3.69%	0.00%	0.00%

Means

Factor	N	Mean	StDev	95% CI
Lisa	14	7.107	3.139	(5.443, 8.771)
Anna	14	8.250	2.914	(6.586, 9.914)

Pooled StDev = 3.02848

Within the 95% confidence level, both of their cycle times are slightly over the 8-hour target. Lisa does a better job than Anna closing her requests from 5.44 hrs. to 8.77 hours.

Interval Plot of Lisa, Anna

Mood's Median Test Report

Data Source looks like....

CS rep	Cycle Time (hrs)
Anna	15
Anna	17
Anna	23
Anna	1
Anna	11
Anna	5
Anna	6.5
Anna	2
Anna	13
Anna	16
Lisa	7
Lisa	15
Lisa	3
Lisa	18
Lisa	24
Lisa	4
Lisa	21
Lisa	9
Lisa	12
Lisa	4

Go into Minitab® to initiate report…

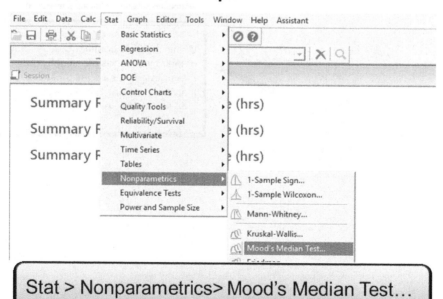

Stat > Nonparametrics> Mood's Median Test…

Filling out the required fields...

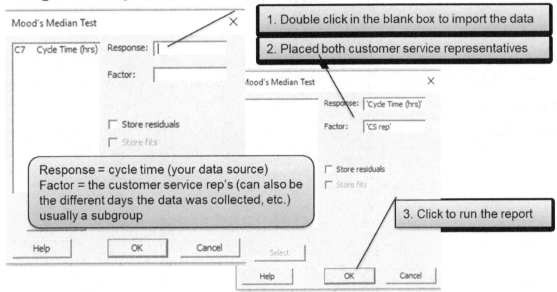

1. Double click in the blank box to import the data

2. Placed both customer service representatives

Response = cycle time (your data source)
Factor = the customer service rep's (can also be the different days the data was collected, etc.) usually a subgroup

3. Click to run the report

Interpreting the Mood's Median Test Report...

Mood's Median Test: Cycle Time (hrs) versus CS rep

Descriptive Statistics

CS rep	Median	N <= Overall Median	N > Overall Median	Q3 – Q1	95% Median CI
Anna	12.0	10	10	13.25	(5, 15.7648)
Lisa	10.5	10	10	14.00	(4, 17.2943)
Overall	11.5				

95.0% CI for median(Anna) - median(Lisa): (-10,11)

This show 95% confident that the cycle time median for each CSR's are within the corresponding intervals. Where the range is wide and the desired target of 8 hours, this shows that it doesn't usually occur. It's more like 11.5 hours median overall.

Test

Null hypothesis	H₀: The population medians are all equal
Alternative hypothesis	H₁: The population medians are not all equal

DF	Chi-Square	P-Value
1	0.00	1.000

Ho = medians are all equal
P > 0.05 Ho
P < 0.05 Ha
In this example the Medians of both customer service rep's can be considered equal

I-MR Chart

Data Source looks like....

Day	Cycle Time (hrs)
Wed	3
Wed	6
Wed	1
Wed	5
Wed	7
Wed	2
Wed	7
Wed	4
Tue	7
Tue	3
Tue	5
Tue	5
Tue	4
Tue	5
Tue	1
Tue	3

Thu	1
Thu	5
Thu	2
Thu	3
Thu	1
Thu	6
Thu	9
Thu	3
Mon	6
Mon	5
Mon	5
Mon	2
Mon	2
Mon	7
Mon	2
Mon	4
Fri	3
Fri	1
Fri	2
Fri	7
Fri	4
Fri	4
Fri	3
Fri	4

Go into Minitab® to initiate report...

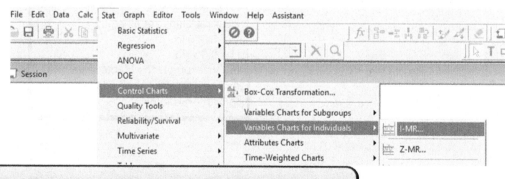

Go to Stat> Control Charts > Variables Charts for Individuals > I-MR...

Filling out the required fields...

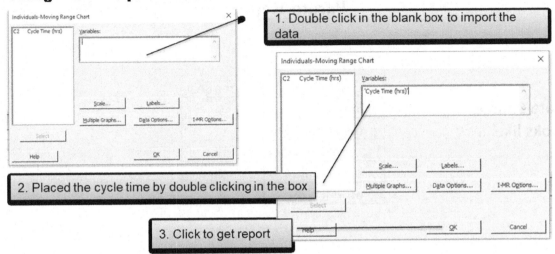

1. Double click in the blank box to import the data

2. Placed the cycle time by double clicking in the box

3. Click to get report

Interpreting Control Chart...

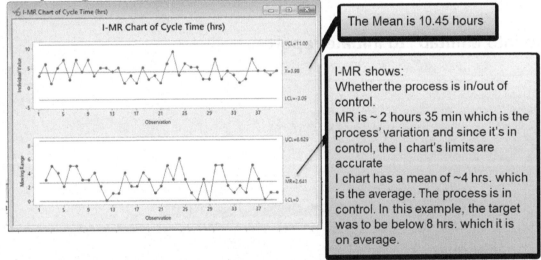

The Mean is 10.45 hours

I-MR shows:
Whether the process is in/out of control.
MR is ~ 2 hours 35 min which is the process' variation and since it's in control, the I chart's limits are accurate
I chart has a mean of ~4 hrs. which is the average. The process is in control. In this example, the target was to be below 8 hrs. which it is on average.

Process is in Control. Minitab will color code dot(s) in RED if process is found to be Out of Control. See Chapter 34 for the Control Charts Guidelines.

Pareto Report

**Data Source
looks like....**

Issue Type	no. request
damaged product	3
product delivery	11
incomplete order	17
order status	13
product info	4

Go into Minitab® to initiate report...

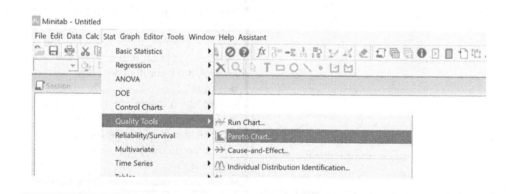

Go to Stat> Quality Tools > Pareto Chart...

Filling out the required fields...

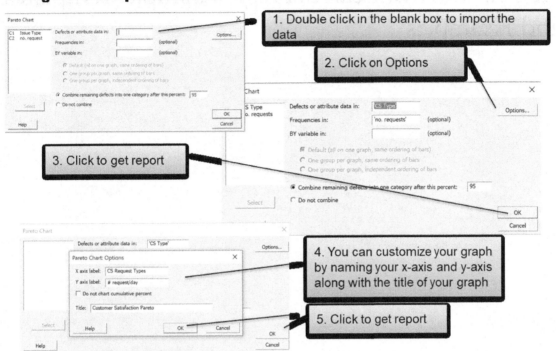

1. Double click in the blank box to import the data

2. Click on Options

3. Click to get report

4. You can customize your graph by naming your x-axis and y-axis along with the title of your graph

5. Click to get report

Interpreting Pareto Chart...

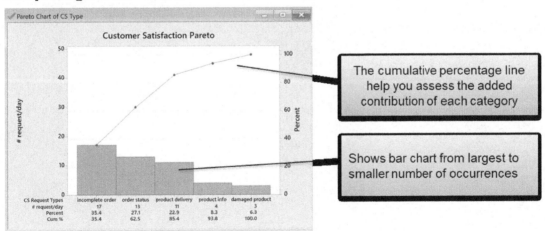

The cumulative percentage line help you assess the added contribution of each category

Shows bar chart from largest to smaller number of occurrences

APPENDIX B: Lean Six Sigma Sample Templates and Examples

SIPOC Diagram: Template & Example

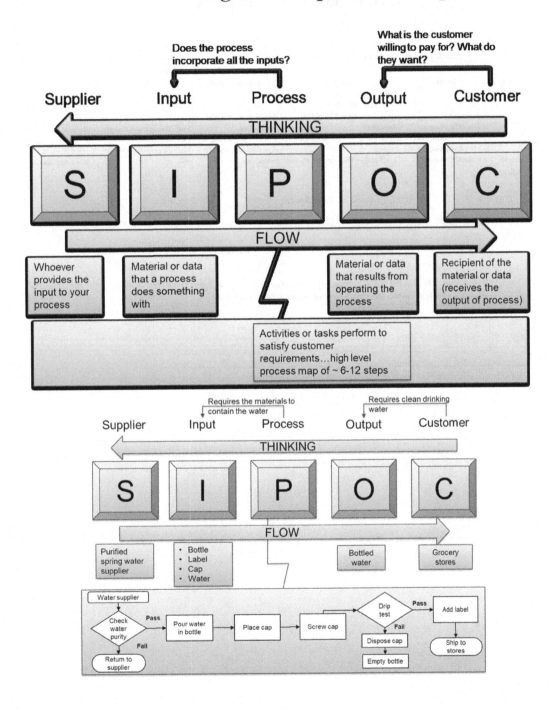

DICE Sample Template

DICE Equation	D + (2 x I) + (2 x C1) + C2 + E = Score				
section	Duration	Integrity	Commitment – C1 Senior Mgmt	Commitment – C2 Team members	Effort
criteria	If projects is: < 2 months, place 1 2 < D < 4 months, place 2 4 < D < 8 months, place 3 > 8 months, place 4	1 pt if – Capable leader Motivated team More than 50% of time dedicated 4 pts – If one of the above is missing 2 or 3 pts – if they are in between	1 pt – if need clearly articulated 2 pt or 3 pt – if neutral 4 pt – any signs of reluctance	1 pt – if employee is eager 2 pt – if just willing 3 pt or 4 pts – if anything else	1 pt – if 10 % over 2 pt – if 10-20 % over 3 pt – if 20-40 % 4 pt – if 40% and over
Score:					

Total Score: [   ]

7	14	17	28
WIN	WORRY	WOE	

If your Score is NOT in the "WIN" zone, what do you plan to do to get it there? And if you are in the "WIN" zone, how do you keep your team in this zone for the entire execition of your project?

Pre-Mortem Sample Template

Pre-Mortem Template

Project Name:		Page __1__ of __1__
Process Name:		
Facilitator Name:		Date: _____
Attendance:	who are the team members or SME's (subject matter experts) participating in Pre-Mortem	

Category	Process Step/Part Number	Potential Failure Mode	Potential Failure Effects
WHAT?			
function, department or group of activities, if applicable	item, step or part number	issue, non-conformance, defect or problem; what failed to meet specification?	what impact to the project / customer if the failure mode is not corrected?

LSS Project Chapter: Template & Example

PM Lead		Project		Latest update	

Business Case	

Problem Statement		Project Goal	
Customer CTQ(s)		Success Criteria	
Defect Definition		Process(es) Affected	
IN Scope		OUT Scope	

Assumptions / Constraints (Top 3)	Target Benefits (Top 3)

Schedule – Main Stages

Name	Baseline Finish	Actual Finish	Status
Define			
Measure			
Analysis			
Improve			
Control			
PDCA			

Project Team

Name	Role/Responsible	Commitment

PM Lead	Antonella Zompa	Project	Improve Customer Responsiveness	Latest update	Nov 14th, 2017

Business Case	Tying to the new organizational initiative, "Customer First", responding to customers is essential to improve our relationship. The last NPS survey revealed Customers find out responsiveness to be lacking and, in some cases,, they needed to follow up in order to get a response.

Problem Statement	Unevenness in responding to customers depending on the type of request. Currently we respond to ~385/day by email and phone calls.	Project Goal	Respond to customers in a timely fashion, satisfying them.
Customer CTQ(s)	Quick answer turnaround targeting < 8 hrs. per response	Success Criteria	Customers feel the improvement
Defect Definition	Cycle time: starts with customer's request date stamp and ends once Customer Service responses complete & accurate	Process(es) Affected	4.5.3 customer service responsiveness
IN Scope	Customer Service group; USA market; Trade / Flow jobs	OUT Scope	IT involvement; project management products; outside USA market

Assumptions / Constraints (Top 3)	Target Benefits (Top 3)
1. Constraint: having the Customer Service (CS) representative's availability for project 2. Assumption: Sales will inform Customers of project and follow thru survey 3. Assumption: Customers' requests are clear for CS to answer	1. Improve the Customer NPS score by 5 pts. (from 28% to 33%) 2. Standardize cycle time to <24 hrs.

Schedule – Main Stages

Name	Baseline Finish	Actual Finish	Status
Define	10-JUN-17	10-JUN-17	Closed
Measure	15-JUL-17	15-JUL-17	Closed
Analysis	30-AUG-17	28-AUG-17	Closed
Improve	21-SEP-17		In Process
Control	20-OCT-17		Behind
PDCA	17-NOV-17		Not Started

Project Team

Name	Role/Responsible	Commitment
Erin Doe	F&A	25%
Mary Smith	Customer Service	40%
Frank Martin	Customer Service	40%
John Matt	Sales Manager	20%
Mark Zheng	Ops Director, Sponsor	10%

CTQ Drill Down Tree: Template & Examples

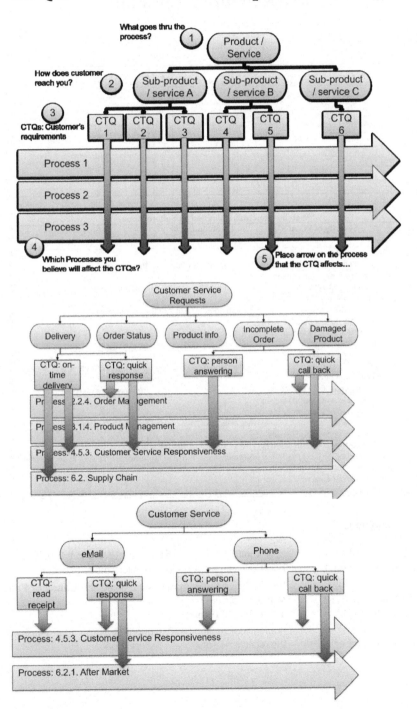

FMEA Sample Template

Category	Process Step/Part Number	Potential Failure Mode	Potential Failure Effects	S E V	Potential Causes	O C C	Current Controls	D E T	R P N	Actions Recommended	Resp.	Actions Taken	S E V	O C C	D E T	R P N
WHAT?					Why? Where? When?			How?		Who?		Action Results				
function, department or group of activities, if applicable	item, step or part number	issue, non-conformance, defect or problem; what failed to meet specification?	what impact to the project / customer if the failure mode is not corrected?	0	why did it happen? When does it occur? what is the deficiency that results in the failure mode?	0	which controls can you put in place to correct the failure mode? When do you need to correct the failure mode?	0	0	how do you plan to tackle the failure mode?	who owns this failure mode and will be assigned to monitor and decrease /remove the risk	What did you do to ensure the risk didn't impact your project?				0
						0		0	0							0
						0		0	0							0
						0		0	0							0
						0		0	0							0
						0		0	0							0
						0		0	0							0
						0		0	0							0
						0		0	0							0
						0		0	0							0
						0		0	0							0

Weighing the Risk identified as Failure Mode			
Rating	Severity of Effect	Likely to Occur	Able to Detect
1	None	remote; 1 in 10^6	immediately detected
2	Customer will experience very minor irritation on performance	very low; 1 in 20,000	found easily
3	Customer will experience minor irritation on performance	low; 1 in 5,000	usually found
4	Customer is not satisfied due to reduced performance	low to moderate; 1 in 2,000	probably found
5	Customer is not comfortable with their productivity is reducing performance	moderate; 1 in 500	may be found
6	warranty repair or significant complaint	moderate to high; 1 in 100	less than 50% chance of detection
7	high customer dissatisfaction due to failure; productivity impacted	high; 1 in 50	unlikely to be detected
8	very high customer dissatisfaction due to productivity loss without impact to safety	very high; 1 in 20	very unlikely to be detected
9	Customer is endangered by safe system performance with warning before failure	extremely high; 1 in 10	extremely unlikely to be detected
10	Customer is endangered by safe system performance without warning before failure	almost certain; 1 in 2	almost impossible to detect

Definitions:

Severity (SEV): how significant is the impact of the **Effect** to the customer?

Occurrence (OCC): how likely is the **Cause** of the failure mode to occur?

Detection (DET): how likely will the current system detect the **Cause or Failure Mode** if it occurs?

Scale used: 1 (Best) to 10 (Worst)

Risk Priority Number (RPN): numeric calculation used to prioritize all risk; number represents the relative risk of a given Failure Mode

GEMBA Sample Template

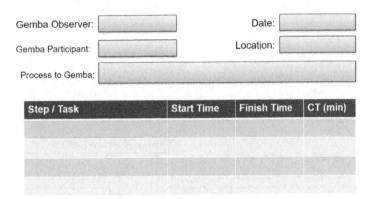

Gemba Observer: [   ]   Date: [   ]

Gemba Participant: [   ]   Location: [   ]

Process to Gemba: [   ]

Step / Task	Start Time	Finish Time	CT (min)

Frequently Used VSM Icons - Sample Template

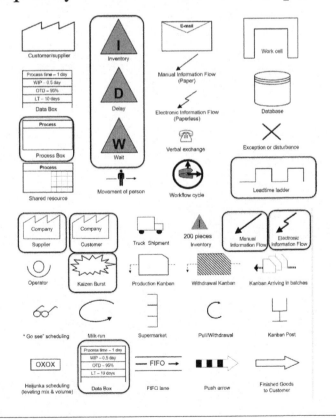

Conflict Resolution Diagram Sample Template

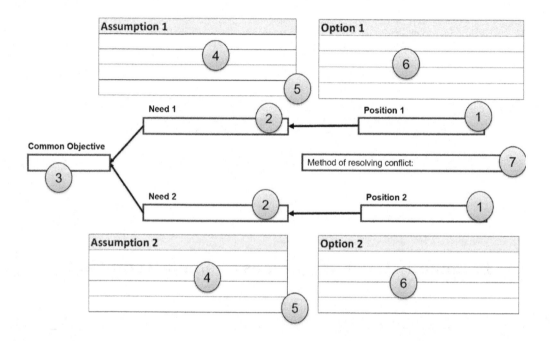

Kaizen Sample Template

Kaizen Title:	Team:
Description:	

Current State (description of problem w/waste found):	Kaizen Action:	Future State (description of results & benefits)

Prioritization Action Table Sample Template

Prioritized Action List										

Project Name:
Name - Facilitator:

Team:

Page 1 of 1
Date

#	Action (Possible Sol'n)	Plan	Do	Check	Act	Owner	Completion Date	Type of Benefit	Savings

Control Plan Sample Template

Control	Unit of Measure	Target / Spec's range	Frequency	Method	Control Owner

Communication Plan Sample Template

Communication	Description	Technique	Timing	Owner	Recipients

Training Plan Sample Template

Topic	Description	Technique	Timing	Trainer	Recipients

Lessons Learned Sample Template

Lean Six Sigma DMAIC Lessons Learned

Project Name:		Attendees:		Page ___ of ___
Prepared by:				Date:

Stage	Type	Description	Recommendation
select dropdown	select dropdown	briefly explain the incident that made you want to point it out	what do you propose to do next time if this happens again

Deployment Strategy Plans Examples

#	Stage	Timeframe	Completion Date	Comments
1	PDCA Piloting	8 weeks	30-Nov-18	
2	Implementation Plan	3 days	5-Dec-18	
3	Management Buy-In	1 day	7-Dec-18	
4	Document Improvements & Control Plan	2 weeks	15-Dec-18	
5	Town Hall Communication	1 day	12-Dec-18	
6	General Communications	3 weeks	21-Dec-18	set up 6 virtual and conference meetings at different times
7	Training	2 weeks	31-Dec-18	set up 4 virtual and conference meetings at different times
8	Metrics	4 weeks	6-Feb-19	work with Ops team
9	Refresher Training	2 weeks	28-Feb-19	

INDEX

Gemba, 5, 8, 12, 19, 66, 67, 69, 71, 72, 80, 81, 100, 106, 107, 109, 114

House of Quality, 4, 8, 34, 38, 39, 41

Hypothesis testing, 91, 100

I-Bar, 7, 8, 47, 142

Improve, 3, 11, 15, 32, 33, 38, 42, 45, 48, 50, 52, 54, 58, 70, 81, 83, 84, 98, 102, 107, 108, 112, 114, 118, 128

improvement, 3, 13, 14, 59, 60, 75, 101, 106, 107, 114, 116, 117, 118, 120, 123, 134, 136

improvements, 10, 15, 18, 59, 60, 113, 116, 120, 121, 127, 128, 130, 131, 133, 195

Kaizens, 101, 106, 107

lessons learned, 28, 136, 137

Lessons Learned, 7, 8, 28, 101, 136, 137, 189

Mean, 44, 45, 46, 51, 57, 74, 75, 76, 96, 97, 127, 128

Measure, 3, 11, 21, 84, 95, 129, 131

Median, 7, 8, 97, 171

Minitab®, 7, 8, 11, 44, 45, 46, 47, 48, 50, 51, 53, 74, 76, 77, 78, 79, 92, 94, 95, 96, 114, 139

Mood Median, 6, 8, 95, 97

MUDA, 60, 108

MURA, 60, 108

MURI, 60, 108

Net Promoter Score, 135

NVA, 5, 8, 60, 61, 62, 69, 70, 72, 73, 80, 81, 91, 109

PDCA, 6, 8, 9, 12, 13, 71, 72, 86, 99, 100, 101, 103, 106, 107, 109, 113, 114, 120, 124, 127, 128, 129, 132, 134

Power Value, 95, 96

precision, 33, 44, 45, 48, 57, 74, 78, 79

Pre-Mortem, 4, 7, 8, 28, 30, 100, 179

process, 3, 9, 10, 11, 12, 13, 14, 16, 17, 18, 19, 21, 22, 23, 24, 26, 29, 31, 32, 33, 34, 36, 42, 43, 45, 46, 47, 48, 49, 51, 52, 53, 55, 56, 57, 60, 61, 62, 63, 64, 65, 66, 67, 69, 70, 71, 72, 73, 74, 75, 76, 77, 78, 79, 84, 86, 91, 94, 95, 96, 97, 98, 103, 106, 107, 108, 109, 110, 111, 112, 113, 114, 115, 116, 117, 118, 119, 120, 121, 123, 124, 125, 126, 127, 128, 129, 130, 131, 132, 133, 134, 135, 136, 195

Process, 4, 6, 7, 8, 9, 18, 21, 22, 23, 24, 45, 46, 59, 71, 76, 91, 106, 107, 118, 124, 130

p-value, 45, 94, 95, 96, 97

QFD, 4, 8, 34, 35, 36, 41, 42, 56, 58, 67, 100

Qualitative Benefits, 6, 8, 115, 116

Quantitative Benefits, 6, 8, 115, 119

RCA, 84, 98, 100, 111

Root-Cause, 84, 85

SIPOC, 4, 7, 8, 18, 21, 22, 32, 42, 56, 66, 100, 178

spaghetti diagrams, 69, 105

SPC, 6, 8, 101, 124, 125, 126, 127, 130, 131

Special causes, 125

standard deviation, 44, 45, 75

statistical, 9, 10, 11, 13, 45, 74, 84, 94, 107, 123, 124

StDev, 44, 45, 46

takt time, 72, 73, 110, 111, 115, 121

Test for Equal Variances, 6, 7, 8, 95, 96, 97, 166

Test Retest Study, 4, 8, 44, 57, 74, 93, 95

TIM WOODS, 61, 70, 105, 107, 118

tools, 3, 10, 11, 18, 30, 100, 101, 103, 108, 114, 123, 125, 194

TPS, 9, 10, 66, 80

TQM, 9, 123

Training, 7, 8, 130, 132, 189

VA, 60, 61, 69, 72, 73, 109

variation, 3, 10, 11, 13, 45, 48, 49, 50, 51, 52, 53, 56, 57, 75, 76, 77, 78, 79, 86, 91, 96, 97, 107, 109, 125, 126, 127, 128, 129

VoC, 4, 8, 14, 15, 16, 17, 32, 35, 42, 84, 100, 107

VSM, 5, 6, 8, 12, 19, 71, 72, 73, 80, 81, 100, 101, 105, 107, 108, 109, 114, 185, 186

waste, 9, 10, 12, 59, 60, 61, 62, 63, 64, 65, 66, 69, 70, 91, 105, 107, 109

Wastes, 60, 80, 118

X-bar, 46, 51, 74, 124, 126, 129

Y=f(x), 56

Acknowledgements and Bibliography

There are many resources you can find on-line or in a library. The methods and tools may vary slightly but to the core they are the same and come from the two main philosophies: Lean or Six Sigma. This book simplified the tools and methods in order to make it user-friendly to the reader who may or may not have any background in Lean Six Sigma. This book does not include all possible tools within the Lean Six Sigma toolkit, only the ones used in creating the recipe.

If you found this book helpful and want to learn more in the field of Lean Six Sigma, here are some great resources:

James P. Womack and Daniel T. Jones, Lean Thinking, Free Press, 1996.
Casassa, Fabrizio, Kremer, Ptacek, Tubbs, and Walker, The Lean Office Pocket Guide, MCS Media, Inc., 2005

Dr. K. Riding and Dr. A. Muir, The Book of Knowledge and Navigator, Version 4, GE Power Systems University, 2002

Six Sigma Academy, The Black Belt Memory Jogger, Goal QPC, 2002.
George, Rowlands, Price and Maxey, The Lean Six Sigma Pocket Tool Book, McGraw Hill, 2005

B. Sweeney, Lean Six Sigma Quick Start Guide, 2nd Edition, Clyde Bank Business, 2017
Burghall, Grant, and Morgan, Lean Six Sigma for Dummies, 3rd Edition, John Wiley & Sons, Ltd., 2016

Dirk Van Goubergen, Lean Manufacturing Value Stream Design, Van Goubergen P&M, 2002-2014

S. Spear, **https://hbr.org/2004/05/learning-to-lead-at-toyota**, "Learning to Lead at Toyota" article, Harvard Business Review, May 2004

H. L. Sirkin, P. Keenan and A. Jackson, **https://sohailumar.files.wordpress.com/2014/03/hard-side-of-change-management-r0510g-pdf-eng-clean.pdf** , "The Hard Side of Change Management", Harvard Business Review, October 2005

G. Klein, **https://hbr.org/2007/09/performing-a-project-premortem** , "Performing a Project Premortem", Harvard Business Review, September 2007

G. E. Singleton, Courageous Conversation about Race, Sage Publications, 2014

Wikipedia – The Free Encyclopedia, **https://en.wikipedia.org/wiki/The_Toyota_Way,** "The Toyota Way - 14 Principles", Wikipedia Press, 2016

Thomas and Kilmann, **https://theparticipationcompany.com/2016/06/5-conflict-resolution-strategies/**, 5 Conflict Resolution Strategies We All Use, The Participation Blog, 2016

Author's bio

Antonella Zompa has more than 20 years of experience in business transformation, project management and global operations. During her career, she has challenged the status quo and helped drive process improvements in corporations. She enjoys working with people to help them materialize their Vision for a better workplace environment and achieve their operational goals. As a former corporate leader at General Electric and Philips North America, she led workshops internationally in the fields of Project Management, ISO 9001, Lean, Six Sigma and Team Performance.

Antonella received her bachelor's in mechanical engineering from Concordia University and her master's in science with designation to Project Management from Boston University. She is presently a Professor of Practice at Rensselaer Polytechnic Institute's School of Engineering, Education for Working Professionals, teaching the Lean Quality in Production graduate certification. She is also part of Board of Certified Coach (BCC) with the executive coach designation, has her coaching and consulting practice, building tailored and team performance workshops.

She lives in Connecticut.

Made in the USA
Monee, IL
24 March 2020